D0103618

No Such Thing as Small Talk

7 Keys to Understanding German Business Culture

By Melissa Lamson

Foreword by Astrid Frohloff

20660 Stevens Creek Blvd., Suite 210
Cupertino, CA 95014

Published by Happy About®
20660 Stevens Creek Blvd., Suite 210, Cupertino, CA 95014
http://happyabout.com

First Printing: October 2010
Second Printing: November 2010
Paperback ISBN: 978-1-60005-189-0 (1-60005-189-8)
eBook ISBN: 978-1-60005-190-6 (1-60005-190-1)
Place of Publication: Silicon Valley, California, USA
Paperback Library of Congress Number: 2010937368

Trademarks

Warning and Disclaimer

ADVANCE PRAISE

"As a German executive working for an American company, we confront cultural challenges on a daily basis. Thank goodness this book exists! I can finally help my counterparts understand the way we work in Germany."

Heidi Hollerauer, Technical Director, Disney, Germany

"We see Melissa as a key resource for developing business relationships with German companies who want to establish a presence in Silicon Valley. The information in this book is crucial to helping joint venture partners and investors understand the German business mind. It's a must-read."

Alfredo Coppola, Director, Business Development, U.S. Market Access Center

"In all my years of working globally, a practical, hands-on guide for how it works in another culture would have helped tremendously. Melissa hit the mark with this book about German culture. She not only informs but entertains her readers, too. I highly recommend it."

Dirk Miller, Vice President Corporate Communications, Siemens

"As a Chinese-American business leader at one of the largest global IT companies, I can truly attest to Melissa's insight and knowledge about the German mindset and communication styles. I've read numerous books about cross-cultural communication and this is a must-read for anyone working in a global business environment."

Alice Leong, Global Vice President of Diversity, SAP

"In order to prepare our future workforce to be successful in our ever-growing global economy, it is imperative that we teach them how different cultures think, feel, and behave. Melissa Lamson's book is an excellent example of such valuable information about the German society and workforce, and she presents it in an easily digestible and truly inspiring manner."

Martin Fugmann, Head Principal, German International School, Silicon Valley

"Fortunately we Germans have developed a little sense of humor over the last few decades. Now we love to be mirrored by such an expert as Melissa."

Monika Ruehl, Director Change Management and Diversity, Deutsche Lufthansa

"Montage Services, Inc., provides international and domestic tax advisory services for global corporations. People assume numbers are the same no matter where you are. On a daily basis we see how culture impacts tax law and accounting procedures around the world. In this vein, Melissa's book, No Such Thing as Small Talk, *is critical to understanding why that is. I would highly recommend anyone doing business with Germany to read it."*

Scott Wentz
President & CEO, Montage Services, Inc.

"Melissa continues to support our efforts to set-up and expand the U.S. business by bridging the communication expectations between Germany and America. Our HR procedures and leadership challenges have depended heavily on understanding the differences across cultures. No Such Thing as Small Talk *is an excellent summary of Melissa's expert advice."*

Gene Dul, President, Schreiner MediPharm L.P.

"I'm a U.S. Executive working for a German Medical Device company. Often the rules, structure, and organization of a German company can drive U.S. firms crazy and make them wonder how they are supposed to compete. Every time we have the thought "they do that just to annoy us," we fall back to training and advice from Melissa and realize that it's just part of German business culture. No Such Thing as Small Talk *hits the key differences in how the cultural differences impact the bottom line."*

Eric D. Veit, Vice President, Admedes Inc.

Dedication

This book is dedicated to my loving family, Sally, Howard, Max, Rachel, Isaac, and Benjamin. To Larry, the love of my life. And Travis, who brings me joy as if he were my own.

Acknowledgments

My appreciation goes to Carmen, Heidi, Jennifer, Maria and Joachim, Nicole, Petra, Michele and Uli. Without you I couldn't have done it. Thank you to my Berlin Poker Sisters, who showed me what having fun in Germany is all about. Much respect and admiration for my mentor, Herb Nestler, who didn't let me give up and go home.

Finally, thank you to all of my wonderful clients who have made this book possible! You are the reason I love my job.

A Message from Happy About®

Thank you for your purchase of this Happy About book. It is available online at http://happyabout.com/nosuchthingsmalltalk.php or at other online and physical bookstores.

- Please contact us for quantity discounts at sales@happyabout.info
- If you want to be informed by email of upcoming Happy About® books, please email bookupdate@happyabout.info

Happy About is interested in you if you are an author who would like to submit a non-fiction book proposal or a corporation that would like to have a book written for you. Please contact us by email editorial@happyabout.info or phone (1-408-257-3000).

Contents

Contents

Foreword By Astrid Frohloff

Prominent News Anchor & TV Journalist in Germany

Many years ago, my professor in Germany told me that, as a journalist, one of the most important sentences I needed to remember is, "I am committed to the truth." This sentence, so simple at the time, became my mantra throughout my career. With each research, writing, or film project, I would say to myself, "Remember your commitment, don't let your prejudice lead you, stay away from clichés, and find the truth in every story." Nevertheless, this is often more difficult than one imagines.

Thus, in the course of my twenty-year career in the media business as a television reporter and host, I have come to believe that the best method to reaching the truth is to become acquainted with the people from whom the story comes directly and to learn from their experiences.

I spent five years as a television correspondent in the Near East. I quickly came to understand that spending time listening to the people and their different perspectives was key to making sense of the complicated political and business relations there. In the course of long discussions, I could empathize with their situation and develop a sense of what it was like to live and work in their cultural context.

I had a similar experience in the United States, where, for a time, I studied and practiced journalism. Not only did I learn the American way of life, but I came to understand the complexity of the culture there as well. To my surprise, although we seem quite similar on the surface, Americans think, feel, and behave completely differently from the way we do in Germany.

I was therefore extremely enthusiastic when I met Melissa nine years ago. As CEO of Lamson Consulting, Melissa had made a career of helping people do exactly that—understand each other! She advised highly reputable German enterprises and business leaders, helping them to bridge the communication gap. She is a brilliant observer and analyst, and I admired how clear and straightforward she was in her interpretation of German society.

Out of her life and work experiences, Melissa has written this marvelous book, *No Such Thing as Small Talk: 7 Keys to Understanding German Business Culture.* Melissa carries us along on a descriptive and instructive journey. She explains the Germans and their culture in its many facets, finely observed and highly detailed, yet with a quirky sense of humor that makes the book an absolute delight to read. For Americans and others, it is a masterful didactic piece combined with practical business advice. For Germans, it's a charming look in the mirror! Imagine the impact on the world, if every business and political leader today made it a point to understand how diverse cultures communicate?

As a news anchor, I have held one-to-one interviews with many major political figures, including our current Chancellor, Angela Merkel, members of European Parliament, and prominent business leaders from multinational companies, i.e., Bill Gates, the founder of Microsoft, and Diane Bryant, the CIO of Intel. Currently, I host an investigative news TV magazine on ARD, the channel most well-known on German television for historically ripping the lid off of major political and economic scandals. I see firsthand how culture influences the way today's leaders communicate, make decisions, and create policy. It is imperative that we develop a deeper understanding for this diversity.

What I admire about *No Such Thing as Small Talk: 7 Keys to Understanding German Business Culture* is that it attempts to celebrate our differences, while simultaneously eradicating stereotypes. It is funny, yet poignant in terms of its explanation for why things are the way they are. In our ever-growing interconnected world, we need more books like this one to assist us successfully with the challenge of living and doing business with our fellow human beings.

I invite you to take my life and work mantra as your own; read, question, and listen to the stories people tell you, make the effort to understand, and with that, we will all be committed to the truth.

This book is based on my opinion and experiences after twelve years of working with German business partners. I spent ten years living there, in Berlin, Hamburg, and Frankfurt. I travelled all over Germany for business and still go back and forth regularly to speak at conferences, lead seminars, and work on consulting projects. Thousands of participants from Germany have attended my courses on cross-cultural business communication. I've taught German Business Culture to people from all around the world, including Argentina, China, India, South Africa, the United States, and more.

The book, *No Such Thing As Small Talk: 7 Keys to Understanding German Business Culture* is intended to be an "airplane read;" a practical guide with tips, tricks, and short explanations. It is not scientific, but a thorough compilation of experiences in the field. Names, places, and specific details have been changed to protect the privacy of those involved. However, the stories told in the book are real-life examples.

With a master's degree in intercultural relations, I realize that the characteristics about Germans that I mention in this book are rooted in cultural theory. However, I have purposely stayed away from labeling it as such and instead decided that I would describe the human behavior in more colloquial terms. Nonetheless, I have attached a cultural profile for Germany with several dimensions in Appendix G at the back of the book.

It certainly is the case that I make some general statements and commentary throughout the book; of course, there are exceptions to every rule. However, I think you will find the attitudes, values, and behaviors I describe and summarize ring true in many cases. My intent is to prepare readers for what is to come or explain what you may have already experienced in working with German business partners. It has been a pleasure to write this book, and I hope you find it helpful, interesting, and even somewhat entertaining.

Introduction

It all started with a BBQ, or "grill party," as it's called in Germany. However, this grill party happened to be in Cambridge, Massachusetts, where I was living at the time.

My friend Kath and I were sitting in a pub in Harvard Square, having a beer. We had recently finished our master's degrees in intercultural relations and had been working in the field for about a year. Kath updated me on her job at a prestigious marketing firm and I shared my dream of living and working in Europe again. (I had lived in France in 1989.)

At that moment, I saw two really tall beers being served to the guys at the table next to us. The beer was bright golden in color but a little cloudy. Being naturally curious (some might say "nosy"), I leaned over and asked, "What are those beers you're drinking?" And they said in unison, "Traditional Bavarian beer, Weizenbier!" (Pronounced Vy-tzin-beer). I didn't know where Bavaria was at the time, but the enthusiasm that these two men, having just graduated from Harvard Business School, had about the unique beer, rubbed off on me.

I figured it was a good excuse to launch into a conversation with our table neighbors. "I'm sorry, but where is Bavaria?" I said. "It is a part of Germany," the first (apparently now German) guy said. We chatted on for a bit and Kath and I learned about Bavaria and the differences between northern and southern Germany, different kinds of beer, and other interesting tidbits.

At the end of our pleasant conversation, one of the German guys handed us a piece of paper with an address on it. He said, "We're having a grill party on Sunday night at eight o'clock. Please come." It was only Wednesday, and Sunday seemed like a long way away, but I said with my most enthusiastic voice, "Sure, I'd love to!" He then said, "Now, don't be a typical American and say 'Yes' and then not show up!" Okay, he had caught me. It sounded like a good idea in the moment, but you never know what might come up in between. However, I double-crossed my heart and promised I would be there.

When Sunday night rolled around, I was watching a baseball game. At around nine o'clock, I thought I should head over to that German BBQ before it gets too late; I mean, after all, I had promised. They had said eight o'clock, but whatever; it was a party, better to be fashionably late. I got there and was surprised to see that the entire guest list had already arrived, and, in fact, they had eaten! The German guy who had invited me was a bit surprised to see me, as I was obviously late, but they kindly introduced me around and scrounged up some food for me.

I was the only American at the party that night, and, I think, one of two women. I was quickly surrounded by a group of tall German men who launched into a deep conversation about the policies toward students at Harvard and university politics.

Eventually one of them, a tall, bleached blond, with a quiet yet classic monotone voice, approached me. My family and friends with little experience in Germany later called him "the German-Dude." He asked, "Would you like to ride across the country [America] on a Harley Davidson with me?"

I thought I had misheard.

"What? Do you have a last name?"

Or how about a social security number? What a weird question to ask someone when you first meet them. But he was dead serious, or at least looked that way. I found myself in that situation where you're thinking so much that you're not sure what you're saying anymore. "Heck yeah!" I said. "That trip would rock!"

Much to my mother's chagrin, and against my own better judgment, I put aside my fears of axe murderers and other psychopaths. In the United States, we are conditioned to be cautious about people we meet, date, and work with, we like to make sure that they are safe bets for companionship. Having been asked to do such a thing in the first five minutes of meeting someone intrigued me and I felt that a calculated risk was worth the potential reward. I decided to go on the trip.

It isn't uncommon to hook up with a stranger and travel with him or her in Germany, or Europe in general. By "hookup" I mean meet, connect, and get to know. Sure, you should lock up your bike, car, or home, but in general, one doesn't worry in Germany about serial killers and random acts of violence and you certainly wouldn't worry about anyone you know, work, or socialize with being psychotic.

Also, people from Germany obviously haven't seen the movie *When Harry Met Sally*. Remember Billy Crystal's character contends that men and women can't be friends? Maybe Germans wouldn't see the point about a movie like that because in their culture it doesn't entirely make sense. I'm about to hit you with a revolutionary concept here: *Friendships between men and women actually exist in Germany.*

Now, I don't mean to say that it can't get complicated, but it is true that men and women may hang out together platonically and nothing romantic will happen, ever. Friendship in Germany is about people who find each other interesting enough to sightsee, debate, and enjoy a nice meal; it could be that it stays like that forever. Of course, it's icing on the cake if there's mutual attraction, but if there isn't, there are no hard feelings. *A German man or a woman can be rejected romantically by you and still want to be your friend.* Incredible, isn't it? That's unheard of in most countries outside of Europe.

Dating between men and women is different in Germany than it is in the U.S. and other industrialized countries. Couples meet in social situations, over the internet, and through friends. Arranged marriage isn't at all common. The pair may get together for coffee, dinner, or the theater. They may date for months or even years before something physical happens. It's not common to discuss marriage and kids right away or the objectives you have for your life, and the whole situation feels much less goal-oriented.

I should clarify: There are clues that someone from a different culture may not pick up on, but another German might understand perfectly. One of those clues is complimenting. It is unusual to hear compliments in Germany. When you're standing in line at a supermarket in the U.S., a stranger may say, "I like your shoes!" and there's no hidden meaning here, they really do, just like your shoes.

This hardly ever happens in Germany but if it does, it can be a form of flirting. Complimenting someone is usually used as a way to get to know someone. Additionally, if you go out for a coffee with a German and they say, sitting across from you, smirking and looking into your eyes, "I've had less attractive views than I do right now," it probably means they're interested in getting to know you romantically. Dating across cultures is complicated; understanding the verbal interplay helps make it less so.

I have been told by German friends that it's easier to understand what people from other cultures want from a relationship or dating scenario than their own. I'm not sure what the reason is for this, but suffice it to say, dates in Germany can turn into friends, lovers, or life partners, and the process can be longer and perhaps more complicated than what you might be used to in your own culture. (I know I'm a bit biased here, but I can only really give you my perspective as an American woman, so bear with me. I'm much better with the business stuff.)

I can't compare male friendships in the U.S. with those in Germany because I don't have many, but I can give you comparisons to my family—my brother and father. I enjoy spending time with them; in fact, we're all very similar in personality (frighteningly so, according to all of our spouses). Our hanging out together usually consists of sitting around, a ball game in the background, simultaneously looking at our laptops and reading tidbits from emails or the internet. Or we might eat a meal together (my Dad and brother are amazing cooks), exchanging one-liners from recent movies or situations we have experienced, trying to crack everybody up. (We think we're very funny.) Once in a while, we might hit a deep topic, but our usual aim is to relax, laugh, and just hang out, not necessarily to have an in-depth discussion. This is more common in the U.S. context.

Hang out or have a meal with a German friend, and its completely different. They love long discussions! You'll feel like the most interesting human being on earth. The world stands still; it's like no one else is in the room, there are no TVs or laptops (imagine that!), and you begin to think everything you say is incredibly deep and fascinating. It's the kind of attention Mr. Spock gave Captain Kirk, raised eyebrow included.

During our trip, in the mornings before setting out on the Harley, the German Dude and I would chat over a bowl of cereal, sitting at our campsite under the trees. I would be saying something and my German friend would stop chewing, put down his spoon, raise his eyebrow, and say, "I've never looked at it that way before." Needless to say, I was convinced that I had become some kind of spiritual leader or intellectual guide, and I contemplated writing a dissertation on how interesting I am.

At the end of that trip, I had learned a lot about Germany and German people. I decided I was curious enough to move to Germany for a period of time. I was informed that education is highly valued there and it's common for German companies to offer personal development opportunities. These include further training, seminars, or courses about a variety of soft and hard skill topics. People love getting certificates for the courses they complete and it's considered a status symbol to be certified in anything. In fact, certifications, degrees, and education are much more meaningful than company titles. It's more valuable to have a PhD and a "Doctor" title in Germany than to be Executive Vice-President. In fact, when you get a PhD, "Dr." actually becomes part of your name. Germans change their passport and other forms of ID to reflect this.

Given this information, I figured running seminars and courses on how to do business successfully in other countries might not be a bad idea. After all, Germany, as a major export country, is the economic center of Europe and one of largest economies in the world.

1 Big Talk, Myths, and Status Symbols

It was 1998, and I thought I would head over to Germany for a year or two. I wanted to check it out, learn about German language, culture, and society, and maybe even run my business there for a while. At the very least, I wanted to have a "European Experience." I planned to talk politics in the sauna, drink absinthe cocktails, and listen to Goth music. Actually, I'm kidding; I don't like Goth music and I've never even seen an absinthe cocktail in Germany. Sauna-ing is, however, as common as brushing one's teeth.

I stayed until 2008. That's so long it's difficult to remember other experiences I had before. I know that living in Germany must have changed my personality somewhat. Now that I'm living in California, my American hus-band-to-be covers for me with servers in restaurants, random people in airports, and in social situations with friends. He usually says, right after I've said something and the person I'm talking to looks like I've slapped them in the face, "She's European." The other party almost inevitably responds, "Oh...I see," and looks relieved, as if they know exactly what he's talking about.

My mother also says, often with sarcasm in her voice, "Tell us how you really feel about it, Melissa." Apparently, I've developed a pretty good skill at sharing my opinion with others. But I digress. Let me tell you about my first cultural experiences in Germany.

First of all, everything is written in German! Duh! I forgot about the fact that although I speak some French, and some Spanish, I didn't know a single word of German at that time. Luckily, most people from Germany take English classes in school from the time they are about six years old, so I could ask for the restroom, or "WC" (water closet), or a taxi from the airport, and tell the driver where I needed to go. Some important words like "Kaffee" and "Wein" are similar to English, but then there are things like *Reinigung*, which means "dry cleaners," or *Auslanderamt*, which translates to "the office for foreigners." German is a complex language and once you get over thinking it all sounds like guttural yelling, it's actually quite beautiful. Watch any Hollywood movie with Jack Nicholson, Harvey Keitel, or Dustin Hoffman dubbed into German, and their German voice is one of my dearest friends, Joachim Kerzel. His voice melts like butter and gives you goose bumps at the same time. You'll never look at the German language the same way after hearing his voice, I promise you. However, you would also never know that it's the same German voice for all those different American actors. He has a specific voice he does for each one.

I arrived in Germany on a Saturday and woke up to my first Sunday morning in Berlin. I pulled on my sweats and a t-shirt and went out around six a.m. to get coffee (or now, as I've been trained to say, "A coffee"). This is pretty funny to look back on, but at the time I was crying my eyes out when by 7:15 a.m. I hadn't yet acquired that luscious non-fat milk, low-foam, double-shot venti latte I was used to. Remember, this was 1998; Starbucks was scoffed at by Germans. "What?! Good Kaffee from America? I don't believe it! And for those prices, terrible!" Today, Starbucks exists on every corner in most German cities and you have to wait forty-five minutes for a cup of anything. This is not being disrespectful to Germany. People change their minds. I swore I would never bag my own groceries or give up the service grocery stores provide in bagging them for you. But today, I schlep my own recyclable totes to the store, and about fifty percent of the time, I even bag my own groceries. (This is standard practice in Germany.)

In fact, in 1998, nothing was open in Berlin that served coffee on a Sunday morning until nine a.m. I found this out from my neighbors, a nice gay couple, who were just returning from the clubs because no one in their right mind is awake in Europe at six a.m. on a weekend otherwise, and they took pity on me. They handed me a tissue and signaled that my eye makeup was rolling down my cheeks and I should really clean up a bit. After all, I was in *Europe*, people don't wear sweatpants and white running shoes AND let their make-up run while they cry at seven a.m. over lack of coffee. "No coffee this early, es geht nicht, cafés open at nine o'clock," they said as they dabbed at my tears.

Ah, that phrase... it was the first time I heard it and I remember it like it was yesterday. "Es geht nicht." In English, "It can't be done." I can't tell you what it felt like to hear that phrase for the first time. It was like someone had thrown a glass of ice water on me. I froze, contemplating the words, "It can't be done." Wow, I had never heard anyone use this phrase in my life. It was that moment that I realized there are people in this world who actually believe that something can't work. If you're from a culture where the idea/phrase "It can't be done" doesn't exist, you'll feel the hair stand up on the back of your neck. However, this is the joy and hardship of learning about another culture; your beliefs and values will clash with theirs, and it's not about right or wrong, but simply about *differences*.

I thanked my neighbors, picked myself up, went back into the apartment, and watched the clock until 8:50 a.m. I changed into jeans, a black turtleneck, and black boots (very European of me, I thought). I touched up my makeup and headed back out. The first café I found was adorable and so European! Large windows, wicker chairs, white tablecloths, brass-adorned doorways and mirrors. I could even appreciate this through the shakes and dizziness I was having from caffeine withdrawal (and probably a little jet lag). I sank into the dark red wine-colored velvet banking at a table I was sure was made by a carpenter from Munchkinland. A very serious looking server came over to me wearing a long, white apron. It was as if I was at the Ritz-Carlton and not your run-of-the-mill café in Germany.

"Kaffee?" I asked. She nodded, exited, and reappeared carrying a tiny white cup and saucer with a delicious smelling brew in it. Oh, and by the way, she brought me REAL cream and REAL sugar. It was delicious!

I thought, this can't be all. I needed more coffee than that to get going in the morning, and today was exceptionally difficult. So I held up two fingers and asked, "Two more Kaffees?" The server looked at me strangely but proceeded to bring me two more Munchkin cups. I drank them both in about seven minutes while I pondered what I had learned so far on my first morning in Germany:

1. Everything is written in German;

2. It's hard to get coffee before nine a.m. on a Sunday;

3. No one wears sneakers and sweatpants in public; and

4. Servers are very serious in cafés.

Wow, the coffee was starting to kick in. In fact, my heart was racing and I was sweating a little bit. What the heck did they put in their coffee here? One more learning point for me: Munchkin-sized cups of coffee are three times stronger than my luscious non-fat milk, low-foam, double-shot, venti latte I was used to at home.

The first tip I have for you for understanding German culture is, if you're going to do business in Germany regularly, learn a few words of German (*at least*). It will make your life much easier. The first time I drove in Germany, I thought *Ausfahrt* was some giant city that all exits off the highway led to eventually... until I learned it means "exit." You also want to make sure you don't accidently order horse sausage or deer steak tips for dinner (unless you like that sort of thing). It's helpful to know if your German business partners think you're a complete idiot or not. The word *Quatsch* is important (pronounced: K-votch), if you hear it, it means they think you're full of baloney. I'm not trying to be a know-it-all; learning German was a long and hard journey for me, and I'm far from perfect at it today. However, learning at least a bit of the language is essential to doing business effectively in Germany.

In fact, one of my most embarrassing moments happened one day at the gym (or "fitness studio," as it is called in English by native German-speakers). I was with some

German friends and we had just finished a hard workout. We were showered and changed and decided to sit down for a protein shake at the gym's cafe. Trying to be clever and practice my German a bit, I asked them, "*Sind Sie noch Spitz?*" What I meant to ask was, "*Schwitzen Sie noch?*" which means, "Are you still sweating?" But instead, what I asked was, "Are you still heated up?" *Spitz* in German means, "heated up in a romantic way." Needless to say, the people sitting around us gave us weird looks and my German friends burst out laughing.

I lived in Germany for a total of ten years. Coincidentally, the bulk of my business there was to teach people from Germany about how to work successfully with American business partners, and then, as I got to know German culture, vice versa. I worked with large and small companies, multinationals and subsidiaries, individuals relocating to Germany (or the United States), and the German government right at the start of George W. Bush's first term in office.

I wish I could write about my experiences with the government, but I don't want to disappear without a trace right after this book is published. Suffice it to say, "Politicians are people, too, and people drink a lot." Politics is the number one small talk topic, which actually isn't small at all. Basically, there is very little "small talk" in Germany. The attitude is, if it's not really worth talking about, then don't talk about it at all. People prefer to speak about something meaningful, juicy, and truly interesting. Chatting about the weather, your family, and sports are acceptable, but not as common, wanted, or needed as in other countries to develop a good working relationship.

I landed in Frankfurt recently on a flight that was delayed. As I was waiting for my bag to come down off the carousel, I looked around, tried to make eye contact with anyone in the vicinity, smirked, and said out loud to no one in particular, "I hope the bags made it from San Francisco." A German woman next to me asked, "Are you from San Francisco?"

"Yes," I said.

She then asked, "What do you think about Arnold Schwarzenegger's policies on the environment?"

That's how it is in Germany. Why make small talk about arriving bags, when you can spar about environmental policy? That's the good stuff. If you do it well, you'll win respect from your German counterparts. In fact, if the people from Germany you meet *only* speak about the weather, hobbies, and family, it might mean they're trying to keep you at a distance, or perhaps they don't really find you interesting enough to spar with.

Another lesson: there is no small talk in Germany. It's all "big talk." And if they start "big talking" with you, you should be flattered. It's a sign they like and respect you.

Life in Germany is in many ways completely different from what one might expect, but in some ways, it's exactly the same as one might expect. I've chosen a few themes or better yet, *myths*, that I've heard non-Germans inquire about frequently over the years:

1. **They don't feel badly about the Holocaust**. Not true! (For people from Germany out there reading this book, I'm sorry even to discuss this topic, but it is the case that people from other cultures still have this question in their minds about the Germans.) Germans are sick

and tired of being associated with it, and they certainly dislike being blamed for it. Once in a while I'll hear a non-German person joke around using the "N" word to describe a rather strict or bossy person, or to poke fun at a situation where there are a lot of rules. This is not the American "N" word that is a racial slur, but like on the *Seinfeld* episode when they called the guy at the soup deli, "The Soup N Word." People from Germany don't throw this word around or make jokes about it. It's still a sensitive subject and can cause hurt feelings. FYI: This is one of the few unacceptable "big talk" topics associated with politics.

2. **Germany isn't a multicultural society**. False! There are over four million Muslims living there, and significant populations of Africans, South Americans, Italians, Greeks, and other ethnic populations. There is an influx of Eastern Europeans, Russians, Russian Jews, and Israelis into Germany, as well. Some people are coming back to where their family roots started, and others are just looking for another way of life. Additionally, the German soccer team got a lot of international press coverage during the recent World Cup as a model of how a nation has succeeded in

integrating diverse players with varying ethnic/cultural backgrounds. There is also relatively new anti-discrimination/pro-diversity law in Germany that is even more detailed than that of the United States or South Africa. The Germans are finding new ways to manage integration and the distribution of resources, as well as diversity inside organizations.

3. **People from Germany are liberal.** Because men and women go naked in the sauna together, those not from Germany assume that it's all about free love, equality between men and women, and an unconventional life-style in Germany. This isn't exactly true. And very importantly, the sauna is the only place you're naked, (with the exception of a few special parks or beaches). A man from Africa who was visiting Germany on business thought it would be nice to visit the so-called "Wellness Area" of the hotel. He quickly realized that everyone, both men and women, were naked together in the sauna, steam, and resting areas. He assumed that if everyone was cool with that, the next evening when he wanted to go to the Wellness Area, he could just walk through the hotel lobby naked and save the time it took to change out of his clothes there. The ho-

tel manager politely but sternly told him, after he strolled through the lobby with nothing on but a small towel over his shoulder and a pair of flip-flops, that he absolutely must wear clothes in the rest of the hotel or anywhere outside of the Wellness Area. So, please don't make the mistake of taking off your clothes in public unless you're absolutely sure it's appropriate in that environment. (You might see some women go topless at a beach or swimming pool, as this is still acceptable in many public swimming areas, but before you do it, please observe your surroundings and see what others are doing.)

So don't mix up the way European attitudes are towards bodies or nudity with their political or social belief system. If you want a general orientation point regarding political viewpoints, whether conservative or liberal, people from Germany LOVE the Clintons and weren't too crazy about the Bushes. (I'm just repeating what I've heard and know, so please don't kill the messenger.) Their current government is considered more conservative right now, but it is still more in line with how Democrats believe and think within the U.S. context.

People are perhaps more politically liberal than in other countries as far as the social system or policies regarding the environment but socially they tend to still be quite traditional. Although, the head of the country is a woman, Angela Merkel, but there is still a prevalent attitude that women should stay home with children and men are still expected to be the primary breadwinners. There is still a negative stigma around women who are ambitious in their careers, and stay-at-home Dads are still very unpopular. I would regularly hear comments when working with German business partners like, "She's pretty smart for a woman." Or "Who is your boss? It would be good to meet him." I would then have to explain that, as CEO and President of my own company, I am the boss. These attitudes are changing, but slowly.

Another example of what I mean by more traditional thinking is that people from Germany like to stay close to where they grew up. They still hang out with their friends from grade school and are most comfortable in their own town or city. It isn't easy for someone to have to change locations for a job and leave the place where he or she grew up.

Holidays and birthdays are celebrated similarly all over Germany, and the celebratory tradition is considered precious. It is important to wish someone congratulations for their birthday or to take a moment and recognize an important holiday. One usually celebrates with sweets or cakes and champagne. (By the way, when it's your birthday, it is expected that you yourself will bring the cake to work or host a party in your own honor.)

4. **It's all about meat, so it's hard to be a vegetarian in Germany.** Not true! It's come a long way from when I used to order a salad for dinner while traveling through a small town, saying, "No meat, please," and the server would bring it to me with pieces of bacon all over it. I would reiterate, "I said no meat," and the server would say, "There isn't any meat on your salad." In the past, bacon bits didn't count apparently as meat in Germany. It's completely different today. There are large grocery stores, like Whole Foods, which cater to the health conscious. Sauerkraut is practically obsolete except at Christmastime (although it is a very healthy food), and sausages are still popular, but not as much as you might think. They are usually eaten for

special occasions, like a soccer game or street festival. Wine is very popular, as well as beer. Surprisingly, however, the country that drinks the most beer per capita is actually the Czech Republic, not Germany. The best way to ensure that you get food prepared the way you want is to describe it as a health issue. For example, "I have a health problem and I cannot eat dairy products or meat. Could you make this dish without any milk, cheese, butter, or meat?" You'll get more understanding from the chef, and he or she will be willing to go out of his or her way for you and prepare something special.

5. **You can drive as fast as you want on the Autobahn**. Be careful. Only about one-third of the highways in Germany have no speed limit. It can go from no speed limit to 80 kilometers per hour in a matter of kilometers. Pay attention to the number in the red circle on the side of the road. This tells you what the speed limit is. If there is a white circle with black lines across it, it means there is no speed limit and you can drive in the left lane as fast as you want. Please know that if you aren't driving fast enough in the left lane and a Por-

sche or Mercedes is behind you, the driver may speed up to your tail and flash their lights frantically. This is a way of saying "get out of my way."

6. **Germans never travel.** Actually, people from Germany are the most highly travelled people in the world, statistically. The average employee has about twenty-five days of vacation per year, plus holidays. It is also pretty easy, *and inexpensive*, to travel just about anywhere from Germany today. People leave to get access to another climate initially, but the culture, language, sight-seeing, and food are additional reasons for traveling outside of Germany. Vacations are considered precious there and are often well-thought through and perfectly planned.

7. **You have a "Kreislauf."** I never knew what this was before I moved to Germany, or that I even had one! It means "circulation." The only way I can describe it is this: you know when the weather is kind of damp, or it changes quickly from cool to hot and you feel kind of clammy? Or you're on a piece of gym equipment and you get dizzy? Or start to feel kind of like you have the flu after a long, overseas flight? This is because your circulation isn't running well, something to do with how

your blood is getting to your brain, muscles, or wherever it needs to be. Fresh air, special berry juice from the drugstore, and rest will help your symptoms. If you travel or live in Germany, or become friends with people from Germany you will hear people talk about their "Kreislauf" on a regular basis. It's funny because I never noticed it before I moved to Germany, and now I couldn't imagine life without complaining about my circulation once in a while.

8. **Germans aren't funny**. This is not true. German humor is sarcastic, dry, and self-deprecating, although they don't hesitate to make fun of others. It would not be uncommon to hear jokes about, being short, tall, bald, hairy, a woman, a man, or a particular culture. Nothing except WWII is off-limits in terms of humor. I highly recommend you watch a few episodes of Loriot, a famous German comedian who comments on German society and behavior in his sketches. He's old school but very funny. A younger, more modern comedian to watch for is Oliver Pocher. If you can understand a little bit of German, you'll find his humor offbeat but hilarious. The most important tip I have for you is not to get offended by humor directed at your

person. This is common and meaningless in Germany. Although it's not easy, if you can adapt a bit to the German style of the humor, please do try! But before you tell a joke to your business partners, find a trusted German friend to practice it on just to make sure.

9. **Business Dress is Formal.** Just a couple of words about dress here: My general advice is to watch what others are doing and then imitate them. If you don't know, then ask, "Is a tie expected?" or "Are jeans all right?" In general, people from Germany are very formal in front of customers or in law firms or banks, where suit and tie dress is expected. However, in most workplaces, business casual is fine. "Business casual" means anything from suits without a tie, nice dress pants, and button-up shirts, to jeans and t-shirts. Usually shoes are lace-up, polished, and very smart looking, unless a person is wearing jeans, in which case it is acceptable to wear fashionable, colorful Adidas or Puma sneakers. (No white tennis shoes or running shoes, unless you don't mind that they'll make fun of you.) Status symbols as far as dress goes are fancy, brand-name labels that aren't too flashy or colorful. Jil Sander, Hugo Boss, and Joop are all very popular.

Tailored, high quality, and neutral tones are popular, particularly in business. Jewelry for both men and women is kept at a minimum. It's considered bad taste to wear a big diamond in your engagement ring (sorry, ladies!) or for a man to wear any jewelry at all, with the exceptions of a wedding ring and a good watch. I was vacationing with a German friend of mine at a beach resort in Spain. At the end of the third day, she said, "You can totally see which women are European and which are American. The Americans all have black bikinis, red fingernails, and big diamonds on their left hands. The Europeans have white or light colored bikinis, no nail polish, and no rocks on their fingers." The other status symbol, more important than clothes (and probably more important than anything else), is cars. People from Germany are very proud of their cars and like luxury models. Heck, they invented them!

10. **Germans Aren't Innovative**. Totally untrue. Germany consistently wins global awards for the most innovative ideas coming out of a country. You cannot imagine the kind of products, technology, and devices that are being invented there. The brainpower people have there is outstanding. Their ability or interest in market-

ing their products, or even publicizing them, is another story. Many of these innovations lie buried in Germany. They might be used someday, maybe not, but they're there. So if you think people from Germany aren't creative and inventive, you are mistaken. It's just the opposite. They are award-winning innovators.

Unless you've traveled quite a bit to Germany, lived there, or know several people from there, you won't really understand the complexity of the society. You may rely on myths, rumors, or stereotypes for your information. Unfortunately, current German TV shows, sitcoms, and movies don't make it around the world into mainstream channels, so it's hard to get an accurate picture of Germany today. On the other hand, British and American TV series are seen around the world, giving foreigners glimpses into everyday culture in those countries. Make sure you look above and beyond the mental images you might have. You wouldn't want to step in a "Fettnäpfchen" (bowl of fat), which means "put your foot in your mouth," or "make a *faux pas.*"

2 Key #1: Seriousness Is a Virtue

One thing other cultures notice about people from Germany is that Germans come across as very serious. When I ask my workshop participants to draw their impressions of Germany, they often draw a face icon with a straight line for a mouth. It is true that smiling is used more minimally than in some other cultures. Sometimes you might see a furrowed brow, and the German person seems to be unhappy or annoyed. Most likely they are simply deep in thought. It is common for people from Germany to think a lot (look where many of the great philosophers came from!), so this analysis going on inside their heads may give the impression on the outside as a grumpy face, but in fact it's not the case at all. They're just deep in thought.

Germans do take life and work seriously, but part of their serious image has to do with body language. People from Germany don't usually smile unless they are experiencing something they really like. A funny joke, a game they can be competitive in, or hanging out with a good friend are things that may all produce smiles. Smiling is reserved for specific events. Otherwise, especially in business, Germans use a neutral expression, neither frowning nor smiling. It's kind of like what one might call a "poker face."

While I was living in Berlin, the editor of the *Financial Times* newspaper (a Brit, obviously new to Germany), sent a letter to Chancellor Schroeder saying he was worried the people of Germany were depressed and he thought he should do something about it. The Chancellor never responded, but I'm sure he wondered what the heck the FT editor was talking about!

Just because by other cultural standards the people from Germany don't look happy, doesn't mean they're not happy. Germany still has one of the richest economies in the world. For the most part everyone has a home, food, and transportation; people have it pretty good there by many standards. (In fact, the local "homeless" woman in my neighborhood joined my gym one day.) Therefore, it's not that people are entirely unhappy; it's just that they are more serious-looking in their facial expressions than other cultures.

The other thing I should tell you is that eye contact can be quite strong in Germany. Sometimes a person is not even looking at you, but instead he or she is "spacing out," thinking about something and you just happen to be in the direction of their gaze. German children are taught that looking in the eyes is a sign of respect, trust, and self-confidence. Most of the time when someone's talking or you meet someone for the first time, eye contact is a critical element of communication etiquette. To some cultures, it feels a bit like staring.

For example, a team from Singapore was brought over to work on a project for a company in Munich. Their backgrounds were Indian and Chinese, and most of them hadn't lived outside of Singapore nor had they been to Germany before. My job was to acclimate them to German culture and help them with any questions they might have about working or living in Germany.

On the first day, I came into the meeting room and welcomed them to Germany. I asked, "So tell me how it's going so far?" (They had been there a total of five days.)

"It's going ok..." one person answered, "But just a little question though, are the Germans racist?"

Putting my diplomatic hat on, I said, "What makes you think to ask that?"

"Well," others started to chime in, "they STARE at us and don't look too happy."

"Oh!" I said, "They stare at everybody, even each other! Don't worry, it could be curiosity or interest or just spacing out, but most likely it's not racism." And then I went on to explain the different values placed on eye contact across cultures and why people from Germany look like they're staring or have such serious facial expressions.

Because eye contact can be so intense, it may also feel intimate to people from other cultures, meaning you might get the feeling someone is romantically interested in you when they're not. For example, one time my fiancé and I were invited to a party in California thrown by some

German friends. As we mingled with the guests, both American and German, a guy I had never met before and I were introduced to each other by the host. This guy had just relocated to California from Germany. I asked, "What do you do?" and he launched into an explanation while making unwavering eye contact. He told me in great detail about his job, career, plans for the future. (Explanation for why he needed to go into such detail will come later in the book.) It took about twenty minutes. Because I'm used to this communication style, I know that to be polite and show that I'm listening, I should look directly back into his eyes, blink infrequently, and keep a straight face (no fidgeting and no interrupting). After our chat, my fiancé and I continued to mingle and enjoy the rest of the party.

On the way home, my fiancé was annoyed, "Why did you corner yourself off talking to that guy so long? And was he staring at you?" he asked.

"I just met the guy tonight and he was telling me about his job." I said. "Right," my fiancé exclaimed, accompanied by an eye-roll. "People don't need to talk that long and intimately about their job with a stranger at a party."

Of course, I started to explain the differences in eye contact across cultures, and how by German standards he was just being polite and thorough in answering my question, but I realized by the speed with which my fiancé was driving the car, that I should quickly shut my mouth and pick a better time to share my anthropological insights with him.

The funny thing is, a few weeks later, we were at another party with a few German couples. One of the wives went up to him and wanted to discuss good sightseeing possibilities in California. She started to explain her interests and hobbies. Later, my fiancé said, "Ok, I see what you mean, they just want to exchange information, but it feels a little too close by American standards." Needless to say, people from Germany do make stronger eye contact than many other cultures, and it's completely normal (and without flirtatious intent) in that context.

Formality in the workplace, in addition to seriousness, is also important, especially around those colleagues one doesn't know as well. Formal greetings, hellos, and goodbyes, are common. Regularly shaking hands with your colleagues first thing in the morning or saying goodbye at the end of the day, although a dying custom, is still done at many public and private institutions. Last names are almost always used in the workplace. Joking around is either done at lunch, in a coffee break or at the end of the day. After work is over, people will relax a bit and feel comfortable being more informal.

You may have noticed I'm using the word "colleague." This is what people from Germany call co-workers, peers, and even managers. Anyone they work with, no matter what the hierarchy, for the most part, is referred to as a "colleague." I have a client, a German company, for whom I helped set up a U.S. subsidiary. The company hired an American CEO. On one of his first days on the job, he wrote to the entire staff introducing himself. He started the email with "Hi Team," and the German staff were confused and somewhat hurt by the phrase. They felt it was so informal that it was impolite. They were used to getting group emails addressed to "Hi Colleagues," which sounded more personal to their ears.

Formality while making a presentation, sharing data, holding a meeting, and discussing a project is highly regarded. Being too informal or joking around may lose the respect of a German business partner. In some cultures, like the U.S., we use informality as a way of breaking the ice or making our business partner feel more comfortable. Remember Michael Keaton in the movie *Gung Ho* when he made that disastrous presentation to the Japanese company? In the film, Michael Keaton is an employee at an automotive plant that is suffering financially and a team of Japanese business people are considering taking it over. He travels all the way to Japan to meet with management and to convince them once and for all to buy the plant. Michael Keaton gets in the room, starts his presentation with a few jokes, his hands are in his front pants pockets and he is extremely informal. At some point in the beginning of his presentation, he shows a slide with a pretty woman and makes a joke by trying to act like he didn't realize it was in there. The funny part about the scene is that with all of his antics, the Japanese managers are sitting there watching him with completely straight, serious faces and don't respond to his jokes in the least.

Joking can come at a later point in Germany, but if you're not serious—at least upfront—you could lose credibility, trust and worst of all, come off as a buffoon.

The learning points for this key are

- Use formal etiquette when meeting your German coun-terparts—shake hands, use last names if they do.

- Maintain a more serious demeanor and formal posture.

- Dress a bit more formally. It never hurts to wear a business suit in Germany.

- Do not joke around or get too relaxed until the business is coming to a close. (At the end of your trip, or at least at the end of the workday.)

- Remember that eye contact can be stronger than in other cultures and that they expect you to maintain eye contact to show that you're listening and are honest.

- Once you've proven yourself to be serious about the content or project, you'll be able to relax a little bit more next time.

3 Key #2: Be Reliable

In the cross-cultural workshops I facilitate in Germany, I've asked Germans, "What's the most important value you teach your children or were taught by your parents while growing up?" The one value that has been answered most often in the last twelve years is **reliability**. What do Germans mean by this concept? Everyone in the world would probably say it's good or important to be reliable, right? In Germany, being seen as reliable is the motivation for why people do their job. "If it's my job and you've asked me to do it, I will" is the attitude most people have.

Getting promoted in a German company is a slower process than in other cultures. In India, for example, you have to create promotion opportunities every three to six months for employees; otherwise you'll have a retention problem. In Germany, promotion is systematic and based on longevity, age, certification, and education, not necessarily on performance, although that is changing. Getting fired isn't as easy or certainly as quick as in other countries, unless you do something horrendous. Because you can't necessarily control whether you get a promotion or not and you rarely have to really fear for your job as long as you're doing decent work, the only real motivation to do your job is a sense of duty or obligation. In Germany, not doing what you say is terrible for your reputation. In fact, if you don't do something you promised to do, it's hard to "get back in good" with someone—a colleague, a customer, or a friend.

Reliability is also more important than friendliness. For example, have you ever interacted with a service provider and they're very personable and attentive, but they can't make a decision, nor do they know what or where something is, or how something gets done? Some cultures prefer that a service provider has a friendly style over a reliable style. The focus on reliability usually means that someone is efficient and thorough but not necessarily friendly. The way in which someone communicates with you may be more important than actually how the task gets done. "What a nice person!" one may exclaim. In Germany, this annoys them to no end—be rude, be bossy, be grumpy even, but for goodness sake, get the job done and get it done well. "What an efficient person!" a German would exclaim, "Friendliness is irrelevant." I'm exaggerating of course. Friendliness is a bonus on top of being effective and efficient, and in Germany people appreciate it, too. But not at the expense of reliability.

For example, I worked with a team of American investors who were looking at Eastern Europe and Germany for potential manufacturing sites. They narrowed it down to two locations, Poland and Germany. They asked me which they should choose, so I pointed out the pros and cons of both. The investors told me what a great time they had in Poland: People were friendly and they were excellent hosts. The people in Poland had arranged sightseeing trips and dinners. The investors truly enjoyed themselves. But things didn't always function perfectly. The driver they used to get around was often late, the schedule got derailed a few times, and they had to change hotels due to a mix-up in the reservation.

In Germany, things work like clockwork. But the Americans joked that the experience in Germany wasn't exactly warm and fuzzy. They didn't feel as comfortable with the personal interactions; however, they agreed it was efficient and things did work as planned.

The only question I asked was, "Do you want to travel to Europe regularly, socialize, and enjoy, and make sure the project is on track, or do you want to make a phone call and get things taken care of virtually?" Some cultures need more regular personal interaction in order to ensure a good business relationship and that tasks are accomplished correctly and on time, while others may not need the personal relationship but simply a clear description of the task and a deadline by which to deliver. Germany falls in the latter category. Socializing is nice, but it doesn't get the job done.

In the end, the Americans chose Germany, but it was tough for them to decide. They really liked the Polish business partners and felt much more comfortable about working with them, but they couldn't pass up the efficiency factor in Germany.

The other aspect of being reliable means not having to check in or follow up in order to get what you need. People from Germany don't want to have to follow up with you to get something they've asked you for, nor do they want to be followed up with if you've asked them for something.

In the Americas, the system goes like this: If you ask me for something and I say, "Sure, no problem, I'll take care of it," what I'm really saying is, "Sure, I want to take care of it AND I know you'll check in with me a few times to help me help you." If you ask a German, it means, "I'll do it AND don't check in with me because I'll feel mistrusted and micro-managed."

There are totally different understandings of reliability across cultures. For example, in Asia, there is three times as much follow-up as in the U.S. Why? Because things are changing by the hour there. Markets are moving extremely fast, and what you needed could be outdated or useless the next day. Therefore, there is more of a need for regular checking in to make sure everything's on track. Reliability in Asia means following up to make sure it's still relevant, whereas in the United States, reliability is, "I want to make it convenient for you to help me if I want something from you." In Germany, reliability means, "Things shouldn't change that fast, so give me a deadline, leave me alone, and I'll deliver."

The learning points for this key are

- Make sure when a German asks you for something, do it the first time you're asked or explain clearly why you might not be able to deliver.

- Don't follow up too often in order to get something you've asked them for. Instead, if you're not getting what you expect, wait a few days and then gently say, "I'm sorry to bother you, but…"

- Set clear deadlines, whether you're doing the asking or being asked to do something. This will reassure your German business partner.

4 Key #3: The Train Comes at 8:52 a.m.

Pretty much everyone in the world believes people from Germany are punctual and like others to be so as well. It is, after all, the German-speaking countries that make many of the best quality watches in the world! If you travel to Germany, you'll see clocks in public spaces everywhere. You may also see a computerized board with a minute-by-minute countdown until a train or subway car is due to arrive at the platform. However, the younger generation is a bit more relaxed about being on or in time, and you may find yourself waiting for someone five to fifteen minutes after you've scheduled your appointment. Nonetheless, public transportation, meetings and other important appointments do keep to a tight schedule in Germany. For example, it is still a fact that you can catch a train in Germany that is scheduled to leave at 8:52 a.m. I watched business partners from Brazil stare in amazement when a train rolled into Hamburg main train station at 8:51 and screech to a halt at 8:52. There is an entirely different meaning of time in South America, and this kind of punctuality or attention to schedules is approached very differently.

In business, people from Germany like to create schedules and adhere to them. If your German business partner gives you a deadline, it's pretty much fixed. Don't get me wrong; it's not always easy to nail down a deadline (the German wants to be 100% certain he or she can meet it—the reliability influence here) but once it is, he or she will do everything he or she can to meet it and expect you to do the same.

Let me tell you a story to exemplify what I mean. I had a German client who sent me to the subsidiary in South Africa. The client asked me to do employee needs assessment interviews to figure out how we might improve teamwork across the regions. They gave me two days and said I should interview sixteen people. "That should be easy," my German client said, "you have eight hours per day so eight interviews per day should be possible if you organize yourself well." I wasn't too worried about organizing myself but I was concerned about how South Africans perceived time by comparison with my Germans clients.

I decided I needed to try to get a schedule in place before I flew down so I started with the most important person in the office there. "Hi Mfana! It's Melissa, and I'm heading to South Africa in a few weeks to do those interviews I told you about."

Mfana said, "Hi Melissa! How are you? Are you feeling well in Germany?"

"Oh yes, quite!" I said, "How are you?" feeling ashamed I hadn't started with this question. (I should have known better.) We chatted a bit about life and family, then he asked how he could help me. I said, "Well, I have two days and I need to interview sixteen people. Since you're the most important person with, I suppose, the busiest schedule, I'd like to arrange the interviews around your availability." "Sure," Mfana said, "just come into the office on the first morning you're here and we'll make it work." I said, "Great, great, but is there a particular time we could meet so that I could schedule some of the other people around our appointment?" He said, "Just come in the morning, it'll be fine." I started to panic a little bit; how was I going to organize my schedule or create a work-plan when I couldn't nail down a time with him, and therefore nail down times with all the rest of the office staff?

Mfala must have felt my panic through the phone because he said, "Melissa, let me tell you something: God gave the White man watches, and Africa... *TIME*. Don't worry, it will work out. Just travel safely here and I will take care of the rest." Of course, I knew what he meant, but in that moment I felt caught between two worlds that viewed the concept of time very differently. Not *better or worse*, just differently.

I flew down, and it all worked out just as Mfana said it would. The people I wanted to meet adjusted their schedules for me right on the spot. They made time for me (in no particular order) and we completed the interviews (some were shorter and some were longer), and I got the information I needed to deliver what was expected. (On time!)

In Germany, schedules are not easily changed, and milestones, meetings, and project plans are planned way in advance by many cultural standards. For example, my workshops with German clients are sometimes booked up to a year out. This applies also to plans with friends or acquaintances: it's normal to make social plans three to five weeks in advance or more. Everywhere else I've been in the world, plans happen much more spontaneously or with a few days' notice. In fact, people used to ask me what I missed most while living in Germany and I would say, "Spontaneous hospitality." Now don't get me wrong, people from Germany are very hospitable, but they want to make sure they do it right, so it is planned well and executed perfectly.

Sometimes, when I was living in Germany, I found myself with nothing to do at six o'clock in the evening after a long day of work. I didn't feel like driving or walking somewhere. I would think, "Why not go visit a neighbor?" One of my neighbors was a 50-something year old woman with an interesting job (at least, it looked interesting, because she was always dressed to the nines). She was single and I thought it might be fun to grab some wine out of my refrigerator, knock on her door, and suggest a spontaneous happy-hour chat. I finally tried it once. To be honest, she looked confused at first, as if there might be an emergency in our apartment building. Once I explained my intention, it was well-received! Eventually she got used to my spontaneous visits (once a month or so—not too often, as that would be annoying) and chalked it up to my "funny American customs," as she called them. Subsequently, during one of our chats she told me that no neighbor in her life had ever just stopped by.

Unless you hear again from a German friend or colleague, your appointment is still on the schedule. *No news means it's still happening.* This isn't the case in other cultures. I've noticed that my friends from other backgrounds will check in a few times—even the day of—to make sure we're still on. In fact, being back in the United States, I've had to readjust my thinking. I'll call my friends, try to schedule a plan two months out, and inevitably get the answer, "Ah, ok, Melissa, sure, let's see what's going on then, but sounds good." Which basically means, "Why the heck are you talking to me about this *NOW*, it's so far away from now?!" Of course I'm afraid if I don't plan it in advance, I won't get into their schedules (or vice versa), but from their view, they'll bump me if they want to bump me and make time for me if they want to make time for me. It doesn't need to be planned that far in advance to decide that. I'm talking about having dinner or something similar. Special concert tickets or vacation plans might be a bit different, but not necessarily.

The learning points for this key are

- Be patient. Schedules take time to nail down in Germany, but once fixed, it's important to keep to the schedule unless you give a reasonable explanation proactively about why things need to change. If you spontaneously decide to change something at the last minute, it will make your German business partner nervous.

- Beware; there may not be any communication in between the time a deadline or appointment has been set and the actual appointment occurs. No news almost always means it's all on track and they'll come back to you on the delivery/meeting date and expect it.

5 Key #4: We Think the Opposite

This chapter is especially geared toward Americans communicating with Germans. It could be for anyone whose thought patterns (or the way one has been trained to think) are such that you propose an idea or a vision and then start working on it. If you see how it turns out as you go along or use a more trial and error approach, then your thought patterns are more results-oriented. Israelis, the French, people from South America, and Southern Europe think this way, as do North Americans. In my projects with U.S.-German teams, this is the issue that surfaces most often.

Trial and error and improvisation are a normal way for many cultures to approach a task or project. This way of thinking is more characteristic of those who come from a country with a pioneer background or whose settlers were more concerned with exploring, survival, and action and less concerned with thinking, engineering, or philosophizing. (That is, searching for the truth by analyzing a subject thoroughly before making a decision.)

For example, "younger" countries like Australia, New Zealand, America, and Israel fall into the pioneer category. England, Portugal, and the Netherlands have a special history with their colonies, which may also account for their thought processes being more along the line of exploring.

Germany is almost alone in the extreme other direction. It's common to THINK about an idea or vision, figure out how it could work, make a plan, and then, once secure that it will work, a person from Germany will begin to actually start working on it. This is a more process-oriented thought pattern. Creating a process that is well thought through means nothing has to change or be improvised. That is considered the ideal situation in Germany.

I'm not being critical of either way of thinking; both are valuable for different reasons. Nevertheless, it is important to understand that there are extremely different approaches to a task that can cause misunderstanding in day-to-day business interactions.

I worked with Porsche when they were developing the idea for the Cayenne. The Americans came over from Georgia and met with the German team in Stuttgart. The goal of the meeting was to discuss the idea, develop the work-plan, and make some decisions about how to move forward.

The Americans came into the room smiling and full of energy—they were excited by the idea of the Cayenne—and said to the people from Germany, "We have the dream!" and proceeded to set up the projector and beam a prototype of the Cayenne up on the wall.

"Isn't it cool?! Porsche! SUV!" the Americans said loudly. "Look at the design! We're gonna make billions!"

The German team immediately said, "That's not very realistic, where is the data? How are you going to build that? Who wants it? Is there any market research to support that?"

The Americans responded with, "Don't worry about all that now, we'll figure it out." And they proceeded to talk about how sexy the Cayenne would be and the market potential.

After about fifteen minutes, they were finished and the German team stood up and said, "We've prepared a sixty-slide presentation which includes data about the risk analysis, market opportunities, engineering strategy, potential resourcing, etc. Let us start to share it with you." As they proceeded with the presentation, the Americans became restless. They started to talk to each other, leave the room, and fiddle with their phones and laptops.

On the one hand, the Americans felt annoyed because the German team didn't get enthusiastic about their vision for the Cayenne. On the other hand the Germans felt that the Americans were too superficial in their presentation. Of course, the German team felt disappointed that the American team wasn't listening to all the details they presented, but from the American point of view, it wasn't necessary to go into that level of detail yet.

I experience this conflict with many of my clients. The way different people are trained to think, or thought patterns across cultures, are commonly the cause of such misunderstandings. It is simply the difference between process/plan first versus process/plan second, or the results-oriented versus process-oriented mindset.

The example my mentor used to tell in his seminars was, "What if a group of people from Germany and a group of people from the U.S. were trying to get through a forest to the other side? How would they approach the task?" He would go on to say, "Well, the Germans would go up into a helicopter, make a plan, draw a map with every rock, tree, river, etc. Then they would come back down and start going through, knowing exactly which way to go to get through the forest. The Americans, on the other hand, would just start going through the forest and when they came upon a rock or tree they'd react in the moment, change direction spontaneously, and keep moving through." He would ask at the end of this story, "Which is faster?" The audience would of course say the plan made getting through the forest faster. "But," he would say, "it depends on if the trees and rocks move."

That's the basis for these thought patterns. In the U.S., we assume a certain amount of change, that is, we don't know what might be in store for us in the future, so we try to remain flexible in order to be able to react quickly. Planning or discussing an idea too much or for too long is seen as a waste of time by Americans. But the German view is if you plan well, things shouldn't change, and you can execute quickly and efficiently.

Again, it's not about a right or wrong way of thinking. In fact, the German way is quality-driven; it intends a 100% solution, but it is slower. The American way of thinking is faster to execution, and it's market-share driven, but it might only be an 85% solution. If you think about the iPhone, we're on our fourth generation now. Each time Apple launches the phone, everyone gets excited and buys it, and a few months later there's a new one out and it happens all over again. The American market doesn't mind that they keep making improvements and launching the next version. We're just happy to get this cool new thing fast.

This phenomenon doesn't happen with German products, although it's changing, because they love the iPhone in Germany. For the most part, producers, sellers and buyers are much more cautious. They're more concerned with getting it right the first time to make sure their reputation stays intact. Launching something at 85% could be seen as a failure in Germany, and the customer base there isn't as forgiving.

One of the biggest struggles companies I work with have is reconciling their sales strategy. Many American companies who set up operations in Germany train their German sales staff to use the sales materials and procedures they have been using for the American market. *It doesn't work at all.* This also happens in reverse. The market needs and expectations are different in the U.S. compared to Germany and therefore need to be accounted for.

The learning points for this key are

- When you write an email to a German, make sure you lead with individual steps getting to the main idea in the end. (Use a process-oriented style, not results-oriented.)

- In order to win over your German business partner, make sure you have facts, figures, and data that support a solid argument for why they should be convinced.

- Know that if you roll out a sales strategy in Germany, it needs to be adapted to the local market needs. There needs to be 100% quality standing behind the product.

6 Key #5: Email Builds Relationship

I used to be really provocative in my workshops and say, "Don't even use email to do business internationally." I advocated using the phone or face-to-face communication instead. However, in today's global economy spanning over continents and several time zones, that's impractical. Especially given travel budget cuts, some people aren't seeing their team members *at all*, and teamwork in many cases today is entirely virtual. Therefore, we have to use email, instant messaging, or texting in order to stay in touch. The interesting thing about email is that there are so many different expectations and rules that it is almost impossible not to offend someone at some point. Who do I copy on the email? Should I use blind copy at all? How should I respond? What is the appropriate time-line for a response? And the list goes on.

I have one client where the CEO laid down the law; he said, "No email can be over three sentences. If it needs to be, you have to pick up the phone and call the person." I have another customer where the practice is, if communication by email starts to create a confusion loop and frustration starts to build, they agree to write "HOUSTON" in the subject line, then they schedule a call to clarify the issue.

Generally, email etiquette and usage has its challenges. But let me explain to you the German perspective on email to the best of my ability.

In Germany, they have taken the way one has been trained to write formal correspondence (on good old-fashioned paper) and transferred that to email. The German perspective is that email builds and maintains relationships and therefore must be written in a formal and polite manner in order not to offend the receiver. (This leads to the question, "What does 'polite' mean across cultures?") It is not uncommon to see "Dear Name," although "Hello/Hi Name" is also fine. The first line of the body of the email usually contains either a "Greetings from Country/State/City" (and you can add "Sunny" or "Rainy" to this, too, like, "Greetings from Sunny California!") or it may start with a sentence like,

Chapter 6: Key #5: Email Builds Relationship

"Thank you for the information/your email below/our interesting phone call last week." It could also contain both. (See example.)

The word "interesting" in Germany truly means interesting. If a German comes up to you after a presentation and says, "That was very interesting," you can be proud and happy. In some cultures, you might need to worry that they didn't understand a thing or that "interesting" for them means incredibly boring.

One continues writing an email by stating what they want to say, leading up to the vision or idea (don't forget to consider thought patterns here), and then signing off with something like, "I look forward to hearing from you" with some kind of sign-off *before your name at the bottom*. Don't forget that! "Best regards" is most common, but you will see "Kind regards" or "Best wishes" or sometimes the British sign-off, "Cheers." If you don't have a greeting (Dear, Hello, Hi, plus Name) and sign-off (Best regards, Kind regards, Cheers, plus Name), you will be seen as impolite, pushy, and maybe even as angry.

I've had whole teams break down over this issue of email etiquette. One example was a small German company with very specific technology that was bought by a very large American company. My job was to facilitate a series of cultural integration meetings. After the second day, you could still cut the tension in the air with a knife. I stopped in the middle of my sentence, "Ok, there is a lot of tension in the room. Somebody please tell me what's going on?"

A German man spoke, practically yelling, and definitely spitting, "The tone in their [the American colleagues] emails is so aggressive! They don't have to push us around to get things done!"

The Americans looked shocked and one chimed in, "What? Pushing? We're psyched to be working with you now. We aren't meaning to be aggressive, in fact, just the opposite—we want a good team feeling in this project!"

I had a look at the emails the German man was talking about and sure enough they were written in a perfectly polite and efficient American fashion: No greeting, no name, just one sentence about the purpose of the email and then signed off with, "Thanks" plus the name. This wasn't enough "politeness" for the German colleagues, and they took offense.

Copying others in email should be explicitly explained because it can cause tremendous misunderstanding. It isn't common in Germany to copy others unless there is a disaster and/or someone's upset about how a project is going. You would only copy a manager (or they, yours) as a last resort when it's absolutely necessary to get a response and they've given up getting one from you. Putting others in CC is seen as a power play, or it shows you don't trust the person to get the job done you've asked them to do.

This phenomenon is rooted in the fact that information-sharing is approached differently across cultures. Some believe that all the information should be shared with anyone who may be involved in the project in some way, and the receiver can decide whether they want to read or use it. In Germany, information-sharing is more selective; the belief is that the giver determines what is necessary for the receiver and therefore selects what piece of information should be directly disseminated to that individual. The attitude in Germany is, "I don't want to bother someone with all the information that may not pertain to them, so I'll only give them what I think is relevant." If the boss or another colleague needs a piece of the information relevant to the project, then usually a separate email is sent directly to those individuals.

For example, I do offsite workshops for several clients in Germany. The internal workshop organizer sends me the participant list and the location of where I need to be to conduct the session. Then they send an invitation to the participants with the details, time and place, as well. I almost never receive a copy of the participant invitation because I am told I don't need that—I need MY information." My view has been if I see what they get AND what I get, I could intervene in case they get a different message than I get or vice versa. Ultimately, I'm the one who faces the participants and therefore could handle any misunderstandings or message mix-ups directly onsite. However, the internal workshop organizers don't see the value in it. "You have your information and they have their information and that's good enough." It may sound like I'm criticizing, but I'm not. In fact, it's really a different perspective on who is ultimately responsible, and I realize my German business partners are trying to save me time and energy.

Learning points for this key are

- Make it a best practice to write emails to German business partners like the example below if you want to develop the optimal business relationship.

- Pay attention to whom you're copying and delivering information to: is it absolutely necessary to put them on copy?

- Generally, I wouldn't use blind copy at all with anyone from any cultural background.

EXAMPLE: Email to a German Business Partner

Dear Jochen,

Thank you for taking the time to speak with me on the phone yesterday.

It would be interesting for me to learn more details about your company: **1)** processes, **2)** systems, and **3)** the key success indicators in the particular engineering strategy Company X uses.

I think it would be useful to compare engineering strategies and then we could decide how to move forward with **[main idea/vision]** and create an integration process.

I look forward to speaking with you again soon.

Best regards,

Melissa

7 Key #6: "I need it yesterday" Doesn't Motivate

I recently had a young woman from India in one of my workshops. She said, obviously exasperated, "When I write an email to my colleague in Germany, I don't get a response for like, two to three days!"

I thought, "Two to three days is fast by European standards!"

The reality is that the workforce in Asia, according to statistics, is younger than in Europe or America, and, perhaps because of this (and other factors), speed and immediate communication is more important. They are used to using social media tools, texting, and other chat functions over the internet. In Asia (and generally among the younger workforce worldwide), instant communication is preferred. In fact, email is becoming obsolete. Instant messaging (IM-ing) is becoming the communication tool of choice now. It is also the case that, particularly in China, India, and other emerging markets, business is moving at an incredible speed, and there is a strong desire to keep up with it.

In Europe, and especially in Germany, business runs a bit slower and more methodically. Better to write an email with perfect etiquette and good grammar than to rush communication. Because value is placed on precision, quality, and correctness, people from Germany like to make sure an answer is valid and well thought through. Most importantly, they want to check or test that something is possible before they give an answer at all. In some cultures, we give immediate feedback and progress updates until actual delivery:

Person 1: "Can you send me that report on the software?"

Person 2: "Sure, I'm working on it."

Person 1: "Thanks."

Person 2: "No problem."

Person 1 (3 hours later): "How's it coming along?"

Person 2: "I'm halfway there."

Person 1: "Great, looking forward to getting it."

Person 2 (6 hours later)**:** "Here you go. See attached."

Person 1: "Thanks a lot."

In Germany it is seen as more efficient to get a request, test it, complete it, and then deliver:

Person 1: "Can you send me that report on the software?"

Person 2 (6 hours later)**:** "Here you go. See attached."

This may take hours or days depending on multiple factors. But remember from the discussion in Chapter three, no news is good news, meaning the person is working on the task and will deliver it soon or by the deadline you've given them explicitly.

However, "soon" is relative! In the U.S., we have and use a sense of urgency in business. I don't mean negative pressure, although sometimes it is, but instead, a kind of pressure through which the intention is to create energy that motivates another person to perform or deliver quickly. This behavior may come from when the first European settlers came to America. They didn't really have a chance to sit and think about how to proceed. They were in constant survival mode and had to decide and act quickly in order to get access to food or shelter, as well as to avoid predators or conflict. During pioneer times, it was survival of the fastest and fittest.

Whatever the reason, people in the U.S. often work better under time pressure; it promotes competition and can create an exciting atmosphere to work in. It's seen as positive to suggest that deadlines are immediate and deliverables are urgent. I've heard American employees regularly complain about how quietly and slowly things move in other parts of the world, exclaiming that the lack of speed can be boring. Again, it's not about a right or wrong way of operating, it's just a case of different perceptions across cultures.

In Germany, a sense of urgency is perceived as unnecessary for the most part. There are exceptions, of course, but generally it is believed if you plan and set a realistic deadline, then you can deliver on it. No need to rush. When a German business partner gets an "it's urgent" message, they tend to find it pushy or think maybe their business partner has bad time management skills.

In the worst case, you try to hurry your German business partner to do something and they rush to deliver it to you. Then, after about a week or two, after you haven't responded, he or she gently follows up with you by email to ask if you received it. You say, "Oh, oh yeah, thanks. We're headed in a different direction now, but thanks." Your colleague from Germany may feel cheated, and he or she will hesitate to take any "urgent" requests seriously in the future.

The difference is in some cultures there is a need for speed because it is expected that decisions or plans are made on the fly and that things could change at any time. In Germany, this is generally not the case, and in fact it is avoided.

Learning points for this key are

- When you need something from someone in Germany, tell them What, Why, and When, and set a realistic deadline. Try to stick to that deadline and if it moves, be explicit and proactive about why it has changed.

- If you need to request urgent attention to a specific matter, make sure it is **truly** urgent and carefully say something like, "I know this isn't easy, however the situation has changed, and we need X urgently." Know that they will push it to the top of their to-do list for that day if you say it's urgent.

8 Key #7: Directness Doesn't Hurt

The seventh key about working with people from Germany is directness. That is the number one description people from other countries use when they describe Germans, "They're direct," or "You know where you stand with people from Germany." If you've just been the receiver of some negative feedback: "They're so rude." Therefore, whether you like it or not, prefer it or not, you will be more successful working with your German business partners if you can accept their directness and not take it as a slap in the face. Their intention is positive! They want to be clear and efficient and make sure you've heard and understood them. And if you can learn to be a bit more direct yourself in communicating with them, they will LOVE you.

The number one thing my German participants say in workshops when I ask them the question, "What do you wish most about other cultures in communicating with you?" is, "Please tell them to tell us clearly and directly if there are any problems."

For example, I had a Chinese client who was working with a team in Germany. There was a status update telephone call every week and a German team member would ask him if everything was going fine. The Chinese teammate would say, "Yes, things are going great. I have a few issues I need help with, but it shouldn't be a problem." The person from Germany would say, "Good, good, let me know if you need anything from my side." The Chinese colleague thought he had asked for help by mentioning that he had some issues. He figured the German didn't want to be bothered or maybe the project wasn't as important as he thought. However, the German assumed the Chinese teammate would ask him a direct question if he couldn't solve something by himself in China. The project carried on, and unfortunately the problems derailed the whole schedule. It got to the point where the colleague from China, feeling he had no support, became extremely stressed out trying to solve the situation. The colleague from Germany was becoming more and more angry that the schedule wasn't being met. He felt betrayed by his teammate in China. In working with the Chinese colleague after all of this had occurred, I had the opportunity to pinpoint what the problems were, explain it in detail to the German team member, regain trust on both sides and get the project back on track.

The attitude in Germany is that concerns need to be addressed directly in order to make sure they are understood and solvable. Other cultures try to minimize the talking about problems and put a focus on solutions.

For example, when you're disagreeing with someone from your own culture, you might say, "Yes, I see your point; however, you might want to consider..." or "Everything's going great! Now let's review the issues briefly and start coming up with some more solutions for the outstanding issues." A German business partner or colleague might say instead, "No, that can't be done. I have a different opinion." or "There are problems I would like to discuss."

Further, "No" in Germany doesn't mean someone is throwing down the gauntlet. It also doesn't mean someone's upset or that it's the end of a conversation. It simply means they're not convinced yet, and the discussion needs to continue until all possibilities are considered. Then perhaps, finally, the German colleague will actually agree with your point of view. In fact, more often than not, if you can make a good argument (with lots of detailed information upfront), there is a good chance you will convince a person from Germany to see your point of view.

There are other phrases like, "That doesn't work," or "That doesn't make sense," or "That's not possible," which you shouldn't necessarily look at as barriers to the discussion, but as questions instead. What a German is really saying here is, "I don't see how that's possible or going to work. Explain it to me."

People from Germany tend to TELL you something instead of ASK you a question. It's a communication style that they're taught from the time they are children. Asking questions is considered either too curious or showing a bit of ignorance. Instead, it's better to state your opinion about the situation and then wait for the other person to present an alternative perspective, if they have one. The conversation carries on with statements back and forth until some kind of an agreement is reached. This is also why the style difference in making small talk is so different from other cultures. Germans don't ask a lot of questions, but instead tell you something about themselves and wait for you to share something about yourself.

In addition to disagreement, the giving of negative feedback is also an important topic. If you've ever been on the receiving end of negative feedback from a German business partner (and you're not used to it), it feels like you've just been scolded for tracking mud across your grandmother's white shag rug or for smoking cigarettes in the chicken coop with your favorite cousin. You feel rather ashamed of yourself. However, this is not the intent of your German colleague, despite the sharpness of the delivery.

I compare the giving of negative feedback or criticism across different cultures to the likes of a sandwich. In Germany, you generally don't need any soft, fluffy bread; you only need the meat inside the sandwich. Other cultures function differently. For example, look at the following statement: "I really liked your presentation last week. I'm not sure the market research stats were all that accurate, but it'd be great to talk about it so we can move forward with this exciting project!" The question about the research stats here is the negative criticism or the meat; the rest of the fluffy, nice words hold the meat together.

Other cultures are still more indirect, "Your presentation was very, very good. It would be great to hear more about the market research statistics. I am looking forward to chatting with you further about this exciting project." So to an indirect culture, "...great to hear more about..." could mean they disagree or don't think the research stats were done well enough. One could imagine that instead of meat in the sandwich, the bread is holding something even lighter, like cheese.

If there is a problem with the market research statistics in a German business partner's presentation, you will want to say to them (no bread, just meat), "There is a problem with the market research statistics. I don't think they are up-to-date." The risk is that if you don't do this, the direct German ear might mistakenly think you agree with every-thing they've said, and in fact there is no problem with their data.

Additionally, indirect cultures may also feel the word "problem" sounds like a disaster. They may overreact as if they are the star of an action movie where all the bad robot-men are about to go on a killing spree. Just because people from Germany, or the German-speaking world, use the word "problem," doesn't necessarily mean that a disaster is about to occur. A problem can be small, medium, or large, but you won't know until you clarify it with them.

Many other cultures around the world think the Germans are problem-oriented and not solution-oriented. It is true that they spend time discussing problems in great detail, trying to understand them fully, no matter how big or small. However, I'm here to tell you that when people from Germany are discussing problems, *they are solving them*. The deep analysis of a negative situation or issue IS the process of solving it for a German. This is important because sometimes other cultures think that Germans never get to the point, wallow in negativity, and a solution will never come. BE PATIENT!

Have you ever had a friend or relative and whenever you see them, they tell you about the same problem over and over again? They've spent years analyzing and talking about it and you've been a great sounding board, advisor, and discussion partner. But at some point you just want to say, "Solve it and move on already!" You can't, or your friend/relative will feel hurt and think you're being unsupportive. This is the kind of patience you need in business with people from Germany. Hear them out, let them figure it out, discuss it with them, and eventually a solution will come. The goal is for it to be a high quality, sustainable solution, so it may take a little longer. However, the good news is that decision-making in global business, as opposed to one's personal life, can usually happen more quickly. There's one more element to this direct communication key. That is the phrase, "No problem." When someone from Germany says it, it means there really isn't a problem and therefore they will do whatever it is that you've asked them to do. Otherwise a person from Germany will tell you loud and clear, "No, there's a problem, I can't do it." Now, this is the important part because in Germany if one thinks there might be a 10%

chance they cannot deliver nor do something, then they will say, "I don't know if it will be possible." They would rather err on the side of caution than to disappoint you.

In Asia or the Americas, it is the opposite. It is considered better to be optimistic and show the willingness to deliver upfront. If you ask someone from Asia or the Americas for a deliverable, even if there is only a 10% chance they CAN do it, they'll say, "No problem," meaning, "I want to do it for you." Later they may come back and say, "Sorry, we need to try another way or I can't actually deliver it as I thought." The value here is it's better to be positive and if things change, everyone will understand, but if not, it all works out. Being cautious and saying it might not work is considered negative or a kind of roadblock to the Asian or American ear.

Let me add one more important aspect: in Germany, when you ask someone for something and they are 100% sure they can do it and so say, "No problem," it is important that you do not follow up with them in a day or two and ask for it again. Your German business partners will think that you don't trust them or their capabilities. In some cultures, a follow-up or friendly reminder is like giving someone a present. I say "present" because I love it when someone follows up with me; I don't have to write it down, remember, or start working on it until that follow-up. Only then, when the other party has checked in with me, do I know it's still important and I should start working on it.

I had to change this style working in Germany, because over there it's completely the opposite. When I first moved to Germany, I needed to get paperwork from the tax office to set up my business and legally start working there. I telephoned what's called the *Finanzamt* or "Financial Office" (like the IRS) and asked for the correct tax forms to be sent to me. It went like this:

"Hello! My name is Melissa Lamson and I would like to register my business and get everything I need to work legally in Germany. Could you help me?"

Ms. Schmidt was on the line and she said, "Yes, certainly, no problem. I will send the forms to you."

I gave her my address and thanked her for her help. The next day I thought that I should probably call Ms. Schmidt again to make sure she didn't need my passport number or more information from me to help her do her job. I dialed the phone.

"Hello, Ms. Schmidt!" I said, smiling into the phone. "How are you?"

Ms. Schmidt said, "Fine. I said I would send the paperwork to you and I will." She sounded a bit annoyed, but I thought anyone could have a bad day, so I didn't take it personally.

"Great," I said, "thank you so much." (By the way, you can over-thank people in Germany, so keep it to a minimum, and make your thank-you meaningful.) Ms. Schmidt hung up the phone. A few days later, I thought, I should just check in with her, see if she's doing all right, having a better day...

"Hello! This is Melissa Lamson again, I was wondering..."

Ms. Schmidt said, "What do you want?!" practically yelling into the phone. I realized in that moment that there was a different system in Germany than I was used. By checking in with her I wasn't helping her help me, I was telling her she couldn't be trusted and making the situation unbearable for her.

I've noticed that my projects in the Americas require three times as much follow-up as in Germany, and in Asia I find I need to follow up three times more than in the Americas. Again, this isn't about reliability or a better or worse work-style, it's simply that each culture has its own communication system. It's helpful to know what it is in order to get the best results.

Learning points for this key are

- Don't be afraid of negative feedback, both giving and receiving—it's considered respectful and helpful in Germany.

- Be as clear as you can, use concise and direct language that has the same meaning to your German business partner. (Clarify the meaning if you're not sure.)

- If your German business partner has agreed to do something and says, "No problem," don't follow up with them right away. After about a week, if you haven't heard from them, say something like, "I don't mean to bother you, but..."

Chapter 8: Key #7: Directness Doesn't Hurt

9 Stuff People Ask (FAQs)

What's with the body odor?

This is a very sensitive subject and it may be surprising that it's the first topic I deal with here, but the reality is that it is the number one comment or question my clients ask me about off-line.

For example, I was coaching a top executive responsible for a multi-million dollar merger between his company and a large German operation. He was American and spent three months in Germany working on the integration strategy. When he came back, I asked him how it went. He said, "Fine, great, except for all the B.O. [body odor], I could barely stand it."

To be fair, the U.S. is very sensitive to natural body smells. I have American friends who shower before they play sports or workout. Wearing deodorant is an absolute requirement. Washing ones clothes after wearing them once is the norm. By European standards, this is a bit extreme. In the past, water usage was expensive in Europe, and today people still believe it's important to conserve water. Although Germans do shower and bathe regularly, for the American nose, it may not always be enough.

Germans will also say they don't like body odor; however, I've never heard a German complain about an American. Instead, I've heard German executives say it's hard for them to work in India or with colleagues from India. In Germany, they are very sensitive to the smell of strong spices or the scent of garlic. I've also been told that in China, people believe North Americans and Europeans smell like milk products or cheese, and this was also not very appealing to the Chinese sense of smell.

Suffice it to say, this is a complex topic. Diverse cultures have different reactions to diverse smells. Some they like and some they don't, but it is important to realize that it can impact the ability to work together successfully. No matter what culture you're from, you may want to do some research to understand what others might expect of you.

Why do they say *Scheisse* so much; isn't that a swear word?

In Germany, "*scheisse*" is used to describe anything that someone doesn't like or isn't happy with. For example, if it's raining outside, one might say, "Scheiss weather." Or if someone sees a movie they think wasn't good, "It was Scheisse." Another way it is used is to express exasperation. If a German person is running late for a meeting or just missed the train, they might exclaim, "Scheisse!"

Scheisse translated into English is "s***." However, it doesn't really have the same meaning. "S***" is a much stronger word (according to American culture) and isn't usually used in a professional setting, nor is it considered appropriate to say in front of children, parents or grandparents. "S***" is reserved for hanging out with a good friend or said out of frustration offline at the office with trusted colleagues. Of course, the word might slip out once in a while when someone is doing handy work around the house and hurts himself or herself, or messes up the project he or she is working on. But generally, it's considered swearing and frowned upon in the U.S.

In Germany, *scheisse* or *scheiss* has a different connotation. People use it in front of family members, co-workers, customers, etc. It would be more accurate to translate it as "'crap" or maybe even "drat" in American English. So don't think your German business partners have poor manners and are running around swearing inappropriately. It is a case of different meanings behind the words and perhaps also a mistranslation.

Why don't they have air conditioning in Germany?

First of all, some of the most highly sophisticated air-conditioning systems have been invented in Germany. However, for the most part, German companies don't use it. You don't need cool air in Germany eleven months out of the year and the one month you do need it, it's usually during summer vacation (remember, Germans have an average of 35 days of vacation) and most people are at the sea, in the mountains, or in their backyards relaxing. Another reason is that most offices and buildings in

Germany have windows that open, which is legally mandated, so there is a natural flow of fresh air. There isn't a liability risk if a window is open in the workplace, like there is in the United States. Further, there aren't very many insects in Germany that could fly in and disturb you. So being a green-friendly country, most people from Germany open their windows and save on the energy waste and cost of an air conditioner.

Additionally, blowing air, particularly from the ceiling is an annoyance. You may hear a German complain that "Es zieht" which means "there is a draft." People in Germany think draft-causing air conditioning from a vent in the ceiling could cause a stiff neck or give someone a cold, so they prefer to open a window.

Why are they so rule-oriented?

To understand the German focus on rules, it is helpful to examine it through the lens of intercultural theory. Intercultural theory is a discipline founded in the 1950s by anthropologists and sociologists. It is a field that analyzes how people from different countries form their common attitudes, values, and behaviors. These commonalities are what make up a culture. There are several theorists in the discipline who have determined cultural categories that describe specific thought and communication patterns. An appendix with a list of definitions has been included in the appendix of the book.

According to the cultural research, Germans fall high in the Universal category. This means they believe the rules should apply universally and everyone should follow them. Rules organize the society in Germany. It keeps things clean and chaos at bay. If you're playing music in your apartment and it's 11 p.m., you'll turn it down so as not to disturb the neighbors. In some societies, it's fine to play music all night long or it's the neighbor's responsibility to tell you to turn it down if it's bothering them. People in Germany consider the rules first and respond accordingly.

Why does standing in line seem to be an exception to the rule?

What's interesting is there are contradictions in every culture. You'd think if people in Germany are structured and rule-oriented, they would stand in an orderly line. Well, if you're at the gate at an airport, boarding an airplane, everyone is trying to get on at once and there is no real line. This is the same for lines at the theater, concerts, etc. In the grocery store, people think nothing of speeding up and trying to get to the end of the line first, and you'll lose your place if you're not paying attention. It's not that folks are being rude. People in Germany believe in something called "Ich hab recht," which means "I have a right." They firmly believe that if they get to the end of the line, onto the airplane, or in the theater first, they have a right to be there.

Why do people drive so aggressively?

I'm not entirely sure, but my guess is that since some parts of the highway have no speed limit, in this context, it feels like there are no rules. This might give people in Germany a feeling of freedom and therefore more daring on the road. There are unwritten rules for driving fast on the autobahn though, so make sure you know what they are before you go driving on it. The main rule is to get out of the way when someone wants to pass you on the left.

Why does eating and drinking take so long in Germany?

There is a concept in Germany called *Gemütlichkeit*, which is described as sitting and enjoying—it literally translates to "cozy" in English, but that doesn't really explain what it is. When you go out to eat in Germany, you may have several courses, but you most definitely will sit at the table for a few hours lingering over the rest of your meal or a drink after the meal. *Gemütlichkeit* is a time for deep discussion, interesting debate, and simply enjoying each other. If you have the patience, participating in it will bring you closer to your German business partners.

10 Don't Forget to Have Fun

Have you ever been to a soccer or "football" game (as most of the world calls it) in Germany or with people from Germany? This is a spectacular event! You will be amazed to see your serious, process-oriented, and direct business partners turn into emotional, informal, celebratory people. They will smile, cheer, and maybe even put their arm around you (and if you start calling it "football" instead of soccer, they'll definitely put their arms around you!).

Festivals like Carnival, Oktoberfest, the Street Fairs etc., are all times when people let loose in Germany as well. I tell you this, because your business partners may seem serious, unemotional, and uninterested in you personally, but it isn't true. It really is simply a communication style reserved for business and the value of being efficient at doing their work. They do like to socialize, party, and enjoy;

however, Germans believe there is an appropriate time for fun, and that is usually after work or in specific situations outside of work or on the weekend.

Therefore, don't forget to socialize with your German business partners, as it will add to your working relationship tremendously. You may need to be the one to initiate this socializing. They will greatly appreciate it once you get them out of the office, on a bike ride, for a walk, into a nice outdoor café in summer, or to a special Italian restaurant you've heard is good (with white tablecloths and servers who look like they should be at the Ritz-Carlton).

Enjoy some wine or beer and kick off a charming conversation about life, hobbies, travel or perhaps politics. (Remember, the favorite small talk of your German counterparts.) Just be careful not to get too personal too quickly. Talking about your divorce or family situation, particularly if it's negative at all, can make people in Germany uncomfortable until they get to know you better.

Joke with them (test your jokes first if you can), share something about your culture with them, drink with them. If you don't drink alcohol, you can always drink yummy *Alko-*

holfrei beer or sparkling wine. That's not uncommon, especially if one needs to drive a distance after dinner. Enjoy your conversations and get lots of fantastic tips about where to travel on your next European vacation.

As I said before, Germans travel quite a bit and take pride in scoping out the best places to stay, eat, and sight-see. They're also not bad at finding deals and are happy to share where to get a good bargain with you. I've had some of the best vacations of my life with my German friends, including the Harley trip, beautiful spas in castles around Germany and Austria, trips to South Africa, Italy, and Portugal. You really should take advantage of their knowledge and interest in exploring new places.

Culture isn't static, it's evolving; I invite you to use this book as a starting point for discussion with your German business partners. Question what I've said, challenge it, and find other explanations if you like. That's exactly the point—*talk* to your global business partners; that will make business and friendship run ever more smoothly. I truly enjoyed living in Germany for ten years and feel lucky to be able to continue to go back and forth for business (and pleasure). I wish you lots of professional success, and don't forget to have fun!

Afterword

It's funny, when I decided to move to California no one asked me why I was doing so. I assumed it was because many people want to live in California or at least think it's a great place to move to. When I went to Germany twelve years ago, the first question I got both from Germans and non-Germans alike was "Why are you living there/here?"

I think there were a few reasons for this question.

Number 1: From a non-German perspective, there are many prejudices and stereotypes about Germany and Germans. People who have never been there think it's a dark and serious place, both weather-wise and personality-wise. (California, on the other hand, has completely the opposite reputation.) They simply can't imagine, after seeing Wim Wenders' films and other such images, that Germany could be beautiful, light, and friendly.

Number 2: Germans have a lack of self-confidence at times. They unfortunately have internalized the negative stereotypes placed on them and one will regularly hear Germans complain about their own people, society, and country. (Particularly the weather.) So they simply couldn't imagine someone from another place would want to live *there*. In some cases, I almost felt they were looking down at me for being there, the Groucho Marx syndrome, "I wouldn't want to be a member of a club that would have me as a member." It was almost as if they were saying, "Aren't you cool enough to be living somewhere else?" That's when I reminded them that Beethoven, Einstein, Goethe, Mozart, and Heidi Klum were all born in Germany. Leonardo DiCaprio's grandmother, The Weather Girls, Angela Davis, and Tom Cruise have also lived and worked there.

I guess the other reason is that living as an expatriate (different from being an immigrant, although I'm not exactly sure how), no matter how long you're living in another country, it's assumed that that you'll eventually go home.

I'm guilty of this, too. I have a friend who is Canadian; she's lived in Germany for over 22 years, married to a German, has German children, works for a German company, speaks perfect German, yet we still talk about going home. We're sitting in her beautiful house, with her children and husband, and I ask, without even a pause, "Think you'll go home someday?"

On the one hand, it's normal for expats to talk about "going home," but on the other it's bizarre. She's lived half her life in Germany, and I lived a quarter of mine there, so where and what is "home" exactly? Is it our place of birth? Our nationality? Where our parents live?

It seems like most of us are becoming global citizens today—traveling, living abroad, or working with different cultures is standard in many lines of business. Marrying or partnering with a person from a different cultural background than our own as well as creating a family with multiple cultural identities is becoming less of a deviation from the norm. For example, my soon-to-be stepson is half African-American and half White American, and many of his friends in high school are of mixed cultural and racial backgrounds. Sometimes I think, what if he falls in love and eventually starts a family with a Chinese-Mexican woman someday? How will their children identify themselves: by nationality, culture, race, or language? Will they rely on stereotypes or cultural norms, or will there be a new cultural identity?

It's simply fascinating, I think. Will we be able to handle that level of pluralism? What will be the in-group/out-group identifiers then? Will we need them? In a world where walls are coming down and going up, I find it hard to believe we won't need some distinguishing "us" versus "them" variable. But what will it be; economics, regional borders, military power? How will human beings feel "at home?"

I have a personal answer to that question, but I can only speak from my viewpoint. First of all, let me just say, I feel very comfortable in the North American context both in business and in my personal life. I feel relatively comfortable in the European or German context, especially in business. I like to think I'm savvy and knowledgeable about parts of Africa, Asia, the Middle East, and Central and South America. I've had both personal and business experiences all over the world, and I'm curious to learn more. However, I wouldn't say I feel necessarily "at home" in any of the places I just mentioned.

In fact, I know this sounds incredibly corny, but this is my opinion: For me, *home is where the heart is.* Don't worry, because I never actually understood what that meant before and I would have definitely rolled my eyes had I heard someone use the expression before. Then one day, when I was working in Palo Alto, I stepped into an elevator and met the love of my life. The funny thing about that elevator is that it only rides between three floors and for some reason you're not allowed to take the stairs. In about 45 seconds of speaking with me (he has an excellent elevator pitch), I was hooked.

That's the interesting way life works; sometimes "home" finds you in an elevator in Palo Alto. Or on a sailboat in the Caribbean, hiking up Table Mountain in South Africa, waiting for a bus in Boston, or maybe even over the internet. However and wherever you have found true love is what I mean about a feeling of being at "home." It's not necessarily a country, a house, a nationality, or a culture… it's simply a lovely human being who makes you feel so much joy that you want to strive to be the best person that you can be. Even more so, he or she makes you want to bring that feeling out into the world to help make it a better place. I know this sounds really silly to some of you out there, but isn't that what life's all about anyway? Love, community, family, friends, security, contentment, joy...

I can only confirm, that for me, after all the traveling, living and working abroad, global projects, and people I've met, that that's what "coming home" has meant for me.

About the Author

Back in the U.S. after ten years based in Europe, Melissa Lamson is a pioneer in the field of cross-cultural communication and global business development. She has run projects in more than thirty countries, working with Fortune Global 500 companies, governments, nonprofits, SMEs, foreign investors, and C-level executives across all industries.

In 2008, Melissa was nominated as one of 25 top female entrepreneurs in Europe and hers was among the first female-owned businesses to receive an award from the German Ministry of Cultural Affairs. Melissa is regularly invited to speak on the topic of global business development and she guest lectures in executive MBA programs in Europe and the United States.

To find out how your company can benefit from Melissa's expertise, visit: www.lamsonconsulting.com

A Another Thought: Pulse Check on East-West Germany

Since 1989, when the wall came down, there is still a significant difference in the culture of former East and West Germany. It is also interesting to see the impact on society and business today. The following interviews are questions I posed virtually to Germans growing up in the former East and West. *Their statements are impressions and opinions and are not meant to be scientific research or absolute fact. They may also not reflect the author's personal feelings or opinions.*

1. **What are some key highlights about the situation in former East/West Germany today from your perspective?**

PERSON A

East

a. Very good infrastructure in the Eastern part
b. Modern telecommunication technologies (i.e., optical fiber)
c. Very often reconstructed historical parts in the Eastern towns

d. Excellent location for economic investments

West

a. The Western part was not very influenced by the reunification up to now; today it is very costly.

PERSON B

Even though a lot of development has happened in Eastern Germany, the overall situation is quite dismal. High unemployment, low morale, social unrest visible in hidden and open discrimination against any outside elements, etc. At the beginning of the reunification, East Germany was exposed overnight to market capitalism and its entire economy was ravaged by West German and foreign investors—East Germany did not stand a chance against those people. It was like a first division team playing against a "freizeitmannschaft."

PERSON C

East: Could be divided into countryside and big cities. There have been many people leaving Eastern Germany who have gone to the West for work. This is especially true for those living in rural areas. The rate of unemployment in East Germany is very high. Some people who stayed might be seen as the "losers" of the unification.

Driven by incentives given by the state a lot of companies decided to start their businesses in East Germany (or move there). This has led to a movement of some highly-qualified people to mainly the high tech clusters (Dresden, Leipzig, Potsdam).

The difference between these now shiny cities and the sometimes grim surroundings is especially harsh in East Germany.

There is still a different level of wages in east and west which many (including me) do not find acceptable. This is one of the reasons that there are not enough doctors, for example, in the East.

West: A lot of profits have been made by people who were in industries that "built" up the DDR, i.e., building and renovating houses, the infrastructure etc. Suddenly there were millions of new customers. And suddenly there was someone who even bought the shabbiest old car. Did life change in the West? Not much. The people moving from the east to the west tried to quickly lose their accent. East German products were bought by design students only, who loved the retro packaging, and they vanished out of the shops. There is some competition for tourists and location decisions—but the old networks and the 50 years advantage in dealing with the western world slowly melt away.

PERSON D

Many people are leaving the East, there are very poor areas with less and less young people, so schools, doctors, shops, etc. are all closing down. On the other hand there are fast growing cities in West Germany. As far as I know the only successful areas in the East are Leipzig and Dresden, there a lot of industry has settled (e. g. BMW and Porsche in Leipzig).

2. What are the challenges of unification still today?

PERSON A

a. The demographic change is faster increasing in the Eastern parts due to the fact that many young people are moving to the Western parts. So, very often just the older remain in Eastern villages.

b. To convince continuously the Western part to continue the payments to support the East.

PERSON B

Challenges are across the board: economic development, political democracy etc. it's also a cultural issue—a lot of people in East and West would like the wall to go back up!

PERSON C

- many people socialized in the "old systems" have prejudices about the others and still see them as enemies

- the unification has burdened our social system (paying retirement money to people who did not pay into our retirement fund), but the situation was grim before

- downsizing of state subsidies is difficult but necessary

- not stopping to work on the past and enable people to look into their "Stasi Akten"

- See the problems that we inherited with the GDR in a historical context

- many people raised in the GDR do not speak English

PERSON D

We're still paying the "Solidaritätszuschlag," a special tax that was invented to support the East shortly after the unification. I have no idea whether it is still used for that. Many people are angry because of that—not against the East Germans but against the politicians. It is still a common view in Western Germany that the unification has only cost us money and that Germany would be much better off without the Eastern part.

3. What are the typical cultural characteristics of East/West Germans? From your perspective.

PERSON A

a. **East:** Very kind and more human oriented, socialization is important, mainly Russian language as second language, less experience with other cultures except Eastern cultures.

   West: Very kind and more economic oriented, personal performance is important, many languages as second, third etc. are available, many experience with other cultures

PERSON B

What might be interesting is my view of East Germans as a West German: I think East Germans fall into two categories—a) those who have adapted to the "western" culture and b) those who are still pretty much stuck in old East German patterns. In my opinion those old patterns are: not flexible, depending on government or other institutions to plan and organize peoples' lives. One aspect, however, which worked much better in Eastern Germany was day-care centers etc. Under that system, it was much easier for women to work AND have children.

PERSON C

What I have experienced in East German working environments (hospital, biotech company):

- consensus driven in the peer group

- very top down between ranks

- trust is extremely important and grows only over time

- work is also "life" and colleagues quickly are invited home and turn into friends

- there are still "open bills" from the past, you might hear who had been an important person in the party or who has spied on whom

- women who work are not criticized but normal

Another example is service in restaurants and shops: East German service personnel seem often to feel very superior to their customers and show this. If they are polite they often use old-fashioned sentences they have learned in the restaurant school (you never hear this from Westerners) "möchte der Herr sich noch mal die Karte ansehen?" "Darf es noch ein bischen mehr sein?"

West: working environment

- open discussion is accepted, challenging questions normal, conflict as driver of improvement is ok

- two types of leadership in hospitals: top down or team driven (younger generation), in companies mostly some desired form of acceptable behavior for the top

- everyone seems to care first for themselves, team comes next

- work and life are often strictly separated

- women with small children who work or have a career are openly criticized

- Example of typical west German behavior: complaining in restaurants. An East German would never complain, but some West Germans would try to give back their food if they do not like it, not pay, or exchange it. This does not happen as often as in America but still—never saw an East German complain.

PERSON D

Personally I think that many of the older less income East Germans are not too happy about the unification and starting to glorify the past which meant less stress (especially if you didn't protest against the regime). But that might only be a prejudice. Many of the younger ones are very ambitious.

In West Germany there is a big insecurity currently. The generation that is now around 60 grew up with the "Wirtschaftswunder," they saw continuous economic growth, thought that when they were working hard they'd have a secure retirement, etc. My generation grew up in such households—we got everything we needed, felt that security and now suddenly, with the economic crisis, there hasn't been any security at all anymore. Many people are very confused and frustrated by that.

4. Do stereotypes and prejudices impact business interactions? Negatively? Positively?

PERSON A

a. Yes – Eastern people believe Western to be tough and only business oriented

b. Yes – Western people believe Eastern to be weak and not very growth oriented

PERSON B

I'm sure they do! However, I have not experienced this. I have worked with a few people who grew up in the east and found all of them to be very professional. Culturally, I do not know any East Germans good enough to understand how they may or may not still stick to their Eastern German roots.

PERSON C

They could impact business relations negatively. I have seen West German colleagues fail in East German environments because the colleagues thought they "bragged" when they talked about their expat experience.

Not being used to changing jobs and careers it is especially difficult for older East Germans to adapt to the changing working environment.

PERSON D

There are still a lot of stereotypes and prejudices. Just lately there has been a court decision that being called an "Ossi" (short for East German) is not discrimination because it is not an ethnic group. The background was that an applicant for a job was declined and the HR person had written the word "Ossi" on the resumé before sending it back.

In my personal work environment I have several colleagues from Eastern Germany and I also work with the Leipzig plant a lot. We often make jokes about the accent, about people having English names like Denny, Cindy, Mandy, etc. that are showing exactly that they're from the East (those names were very popular there about 20–30 years ago in the East and not at all in the West) and such little things like that but everybody is laughing about it and nobody is taking it seriously. It's kind of the same way like we Bavarians are joking about the North Germans and the East and North Germans are making fun of Bavarian customs (like calling ourselves by the surname first before the first name, a thing the others never do and is often confusing for them).

I don't know whether there are still environments where there is serious discrimination going on.

5. What would you recommend to change/improve about East/West Germany? Economically, socially, integration-wise?

PERSON A

a. There have been enough programs in place—we just need one or two more generations
b. We need less world problems, i.e., finance markets, immobile crises, Greece crises, Iran, Iraq, crises—then Germany will be able to focus more on internal optimization and finally succeed with their integration processes, it is just a matter of time.

PERSON C

I would propose to stop to pay different wages and also the amount of vacation days should be more balanced. I hope that the integration will proceed automatically. I would unify the school system in the BRD. It is organized by the state and the children have problems when they move from one state to the other in Germany. I would also take care that there are more young teachers, as the average teacher in some area is over 50 years old. And I would encourage a Europe wide exchange of teachers.

PERSON D

I think it is necessary to support the poor areas and try to populate them again. The scenery there is really nice—I think there are possibilities. I also don't understand why here it doesn't work the same as in the US: I've been to several cities/towns there that once were close to dying out and then artists, hippies, whoever moved there as it was cheap, and made a special place out of it. I have no idea why nobody is making use of that in Germany.

6. Is there a question you would recommend I should have the answer to about former East/West Germany/Germans?

PERSON A

Yes: How to compensate quickly aging matters in the Eastern part.

PERSON B

An interesting question—also to ask west or East Germans (especially in an environment where people from both groups have to work together)—is: does the wall still exist in your head? ("ist die mauer im kopf noch da?")

PERSON C

How should you behave as a black/foreign looking person in East Germany. I have black children in my family and they have to endure a lot of staring when they travel to places in Germany where there are few foreigners. My impression is that there is more open staring and hostility in East Germany. This is a scary problem. Some children in the class of my son did not want to go on a school trip to Brandenburg because of this (he goes to an international school). It is important to explain why in East Germany there seem to be more resentment towards foreigners.

Appendix A: Another Thought: Pulse Check on East-West Germany

B Trivia Questions about Germany

1. How many states are there in the whole of Germany?
2. The most important head of the country is a Prime Minister, a President or a Chancellor?
3. What colors are the German flag?
4. What is the population of Germany?
5. What religion are most Germans?
6. What is the largest city?
7. What is considered popular fast food?
8. What sport is the most popular in Germany?
9. What is the speed limit on the Autobahn in Germany?
10. What is the price of gas in Germany?
11. Where are the beaches in Germany?
12. Who are the number one consumers of beer in the world per capita?
13. International dialing code?
14. Internet code is?

Answers to Trivia Questions About Germany

1. 16 States
2. Chancellor
3. Black, Red, Gold (yellow)
4. 83,000,000
5. Christian
6. Berlin
7. Sausages
8. Soccer
9. It Varies (Not unlimited)
10. $6 – $7/gallon (2010)
11. Northern Coast
12. Czech Republic
13. +49
14. .de

Appendix

C Some Common Phrases in German

English	German
Can you help me?	Können Sie mir helfen?
Do you speak English?	Sprechen Sie Englisch?
Do you understand?	Verstehen Sie?
Do you understand English?	Verstehen Sie Englisch?
Excuse me	Entschuldigung
Good afternoon	Guten Tag
Good day	Guten Tag
Good morning	Guten Morgen
Good evening	Guten Abend
Good night	Gute Nacht
Good-bye	Auf Wiedersehen.

English	German
Happy Birthday!	Herzlichen Glückwunsch zum Geburtstag!
How do you say...?	Wie sagt man...?
Help!	Hilfe!
I don't know.	Ich weiß nicht.
I don't speak German.	Ich spreche kein Deutsch
I don't understand.	Ich verstehe nicht
I like	Ich mag
I have	Ich habe

D Some Common Words/Expressions Germans Use in English

Handy or Mobile = Cell phone

Under Four Eyes = One-on-one discussion

You must not = You don't have to

You must = You should

I wish you a good... = Have a nice...

Ciao = See ya

"Give my best greetings to" = "Say 'hi' to"

Some Common Non-Verbal Expressions

Tapping the temple means someone is crazy.

An open palm waving in front of your eyes means someone is crazy.

Taking the pointer finger and pulling the skin below the eye down a little bit means you're being facetious.

Nodding your head back and forth sideways and moving your hand in the same way means you're not sure if you agree with what someone is saying.

E Useful Websites about German Society

About Germany

http://en.wikipedia.org/wiki/Germany

http://bit.ly/dkcoum [1]

German Beer

http://www.germanbeerinstitute.com/

German Food

http://www.kitchenproject.com/german/

Traveling to Germany

http://bit.ly/9y6XpL [2]

---

1. www.infoplease.com/ipa/A0107568.html #axzz0zyXWG
2. www.germanculture.com.ua/library/links/travel.htm

Soccer Rules

http://bit.ly/8Zi73H [3]

Shopping in Germany (Christmas Markets)

http://www.germany-christmas-market.org.uk/

Driving in Germany

http://www.howtogermany.com/pages/driving.html

---

3. www.soccerhelp.com/Soccer_Rules_Rules_Of_Soccer.shtml

F Business Resources for Germany

German Chambers of Commerce (IHK)

http://www.frankfurt-main.ihk.de/english/

http://bit.ly/bZquw0 [4]

German-American Business Association

http://www.gaba-network.org/

American German Business Club

http://www.agbc.de/index.php?home

Germany Career Center

http://www.germany-usa.com/

---

4. www.gaccphiladelphia.com/index.php?id=82&L=15

Invest in Germany

http://www.gtai.com/web_en/homepage

German Business Law

http://www.germanlawjournal.com/

G Definitions of the Cultural Profile Dimensions

According to the research that Lamson Consulting, LLC has done in the form of interviews, polling and analysis over a 12 year time-span, the Cultural Profile for Germany has been determined to be (specific values have not been included):

Universal, Individual, Specific, Internal, Monochronic, Deductive, and Low Context

Definitions of the Cultural Profile Dimensions*:

1. **Universal** – Accountability and consistency to rules, beliefs and procedures is highly valued. Rules apply equally.

   Particular – Accountability to relationships is primary. Rules change and are adjustable to the situation and the people involved.

2. **Individual** – Encourages individual freedom and responsibility. Personal expression and individual initiative is valued. Individual people are less hierarchy-oriented.

Collective – Encourages individuals to work for consensus in the interest of the group. The values of the group and its survival are primary. Collective people are more hierarchy-oriented.

3. **Specific** – Business is separate from other aspects of life. Clear lines of differentiation and separation exist between all aspects of life.

   Diffuse – The integration of all aspects of personal and professional life can stabilize and create success. Everything is connected.

4. **Internal** – Nature can be controlled once it is understood. People can and should influence their environment, not vice versa.

   External – People are subjugated to all of the environment's dynamic and forces. Unpredictable things like luck, fate, change, etc. determine the cause of events.

5. **Monochronic** – time can be controlled. Schedules should be made and followed. Efficiency is more important than relationships.

   Polychronic – time cannot be controlled. Schedules should be flexible and relationships are more important than keeping appointments.

6. **Inductive** – thinking patterns start with a vision, suggest it, and then figure out how to execute.

   Deductive – thinking patterns start with a plan, or way to execute an idea, suggest it, then talk about the vision.

7. **Low Context** – direct communication is appreciated, written words are taken seriously, what you say is what you mean.

    High Context – indirect communication is appreciated, spoken words build trust, relationship is more important that words.

*A definition list created by Melissa Lamson for her course materials on working across cultures. Based on the work of Fons Trompenaars and Edward Hall.**

References

Adler, Nancy. *International Dimensions of Organizational Behavior.* Cincinnati, Ohio: South-Western College Publishing, 1997.

Bennett, Milton, Ed. *Basic Concepts of Intercultural Communication.* Yarmouth, Maine: Intercultural Press, 1998.

Hall, Edward. *The Hidden Dimension & The Silent Language.* New York: John Wiley & Sons, 1990.

Hofstede, Geert. *Culture's Consequences: Comparing Values, Behaviors, Institutions, and Organizations across Nations.* Sage Publications, 2001.

Interview with Melissa Lamson. (2007). "Team Player." *Talent Management in Germany and the United States.*

Lamson, Melissa. (2000). "Style-Switching: A Critical Success Factor in German-American Business Interface." *American Chamber of Commerce.*

Lamson, Melissa. (2001). "Cultural Considerations for American Managers in Germany." *American Chamber of Commerce.*

Melissa Lamson Interview. (2001). "Aspects of Intercultural Training." *Global Player.*

Lamson, Melissa. (2002). "Political Correctness." *Sietar Journal.* Interview with Melissa Lamson. (2006). "The Continental Divide." *SAPWorld.*

Trompenaars, Fons & Hampden-Turner, Charles. *Riding the Waves of Culture: Understanding Cultural Diversity in Business.* London: Nicolas Brealey Publishing Limited, 2008.

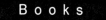

Other Happy About® Books

Purchase these books at Happy About http://happyabout.info or at other online and physical bookstores.

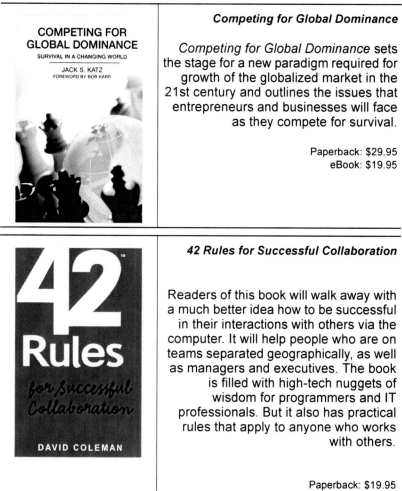

COMPETING FOR GLOBAL DOMINANCE
SURVIVAL IN A CHANGING WORLD
JACK S. KATZ
FOREWORD BY BOB KARR

Competing for Global Dominance

Competing for Global Dominance sets the stage for a new paradigm required for growth of the globalized market in the 21st century and outlines the issues that entrepreneurs and businesses will face as they compete for survival.

Paperback: $29.95
eBook: $19.95

42 Rules
for Successful Collaboration
DAVID COLEMAN

42 Rules for Successful Collaboration

Readers of this book will walk away with a much better idea how to be successful in their interactions with others via the computer. It will help people who are on teams separated geographically, as well as managers and executives. The book is filled with high-tech nuggets of wisdom for programmers and IT professionals. But it also has practical rules that apply to anyone who works with others.

Paperback: $19.95
eBook: $14.95

Scrappy Women in Business

This refreshingly honest book provides welcome reassurance for every businesswoman who's ever wondered, "Is it me, or has the whole rest of the company gone nuts?!"

Paperback: $19.95
eBook: $14.95

#PARTNER tweet Book01

This book helps you increase your profitability through understanding the most powerful approach to smart partnerships, and offers practical tips and advice to give you competitive advantage.

Paperback: $19.95
eBook: $14.95

CPSIA information can be obtained at www.ICGtesting.com
Printed in the USA
BVOW05s1259240414

351605BV00007B/156/P